# SUPER EASY CARNIVORE DIET AIR FRYER COOKBOOK

*A Feast of Delicious, Protein-Rich, Low-Carb Recipes You Can Whip Up in a Flash – Boost Energy, Shed Pounds, and Improve Your Health!*

Joshua Michael Davis

# TABLE OF CONTENTS

**Chapter 6: Special Occasion Feasts**

# Chapter 1: Carnivore Diet Air Fryer Cookbook: Introduction

Welcome to a world where the simplicity of meat meets the innovation of air frying, a culinary duo ready to revolutionize your kitchen and your health. As you embark on this flavorful journey, you're not just flipping through another cookbook; you're unlocking the door to a lifestyle that champions high-protein, nutrient-dense meals without the fuss of traditional cooking methods. The Carnivore Diet Air Fryer Cookbook is not about conforming to the standard dietary guidelines that have long dictated our eating habits. Instead, it's about challenging the status quo, embracing a meat-centric diet, and discovering the transformative power of air frying to make each meal not just a feast for the taste buds but a building block for better health.

The Carnivore Diet strips away the complexities of modern diets, focusing on the primal, nutrient-rich foods that our ancestors thrived on. Meat, in all its forms, becomes the star of the show, providing everything your body needs to function optimally—protein, fats, and essential vitamins and minerals. But let's face it, diving into a meat-only diet can seem daunting at first. How do you keep meals exciting? How do you ensure each dish is cooked to perfection without spending hours in the kitchen? That's where your air fryer comes in, a modern kitchen miracle that can transform even the simplest cut of meat into a crispy, juicy masterpiece in minutes.

This book is designed with you in mind—the busy, health-conscious individual who juggles work, family, and a bustling household. You're looking for ways to streamline your cooking process without sacrificing flavor or nutritional value. You're curious about the Carnivore Diet but need practical advice on how to integrate it into your daily routine. You're in search of a collection of recipes that go beyond the basic steak and eggs, offering variety and excitement for every meal of the day. And most importantly, you're eager to embark on a dietary adventure that promises to enhance your health, energy, and well-being.

From understanding the fundamental principles of the Carnivore Diet to mastering the art of air frying, this book covers it all. You'll learn about the different cuts of meat and how to select the best ones for air frying. You'll discover the secrets to achieving the perfect texture and flavor, whether you're cooking a tender filet mignon or crispy chicken wings. You'll be equipped with over 200 carnivore-approved recipes that showcase the versatility and deliciousness of a meat-centric diet. And through it all, you'll be guided by clear, step-by-step instructions that make cooking with your air fryer a breeze.

But this book is more than just a collection of recipes. It's a comprehensive guide to transforming your health through the foods you eat. You'll explore the science behind the Carnivore Diet, including its potential benefits for weight loss, inflammation reduction, and mental health stabilization. You'll read real-life success stories from individuals who have experienced dramatic health transformations by adopting a meat-based diet. And you'll find practical tips for navigating common challenges, making sustainable dietary changes, and staying motivated on your carnivore journey.

So, whether you're a seasoned carnivore enthusiast or a curious newcomer, the Carnivore Diet Air Fryer Cookbook is your ultimate resource for delicious, nutritious, and effortlessly prepared meals. Say goodbye to the days of boring, repetitive meals and hello to a world of flavor, variety, and health benefits. Your air fryer is about to become your best friend in the kitchen, and together, you'll unlock the full potential of a carnivore diet that's not just sustainable but truly enjoyable. Let's get cooking!

# Embracing the Carnivore Lifestyle

Switching to a carnivore lifestyle might seem like a bold leap from traditional dietary patterns, but it's a step toward reclaiming your health, vitality, and culinary enjoyment. This lifestyle is not just about eating meat; it's about nourishing your body with high-quality, nutrient-dense foods that align with human biology. The carnivore diet simplifies eating by focusing on animal products, eliminating the guesswork and complexity often associated with modern diets laden with processed foods, grains, and sugars. It's about getting back to basics, where meals are straightforward yet profoundly satisfying.

For those new to this way of eating, the concept might raise eyebrows. You might wonder how you can sustain yourself on meat alone. However, countless anecdotes and emerging studies suggest that a meat-focused diet can support various aspects of health, from enhancing mental clarity and energy levels to reducing inflammation and aiding in weight management. The key is to select high-quality meats, including beef, poultry, fish, and organ meats, which provide a spectrum of nutrients essential for optimal health.

Embracing the carnivore lifestyle means rethinking conventional wisdom about nutrition. It involves questioning the dietary guidelines that have long promoted a high-carb, low-fat diet as the path to health. Instead, you'll explore how consuming animal products exclusively can lead to improvements in health markers, such as blood sugar levels, lipid profiles, and blood pressure. It's a journey of discovery, where you'll learn to listen to your body and adjust your diet based on how you feel and the health outcomes you experience.

One of the most appealing aspects of the carnivore diet is its simplicity. No complicated recipes, portion control, or calorie counting are required. Your meals will revolve around meat, with the option to include eggs, dairy, and fish, depending on your personal preference and tolerance. This simplicity is a boon for busy individuals seeking nutritious, satisfying meals without spending hours in the kitchen. And with the air fryer, you can prepare delicious, crispy, and juicy meats with minimal effort, making it easier to stick to this lifestyle.

However, adopting a carnivore diet doesn't mean you'll never face challenges or doubts. You may encounter skepticism from friends and family or navigate social situations where plant-based foods are the norm. But armed with knowledge and a clear understanding of the benefits you're seeking, you can confidently embrace the carnivore lifestyle. It's about making informed choices that support your health goals, whether you're looking to improve specific health conditions, optimize your physical performance, or simply feel better in your daily life.

Remember, transitioning to a carnivore diet is a personal journey that can be adapted to fit your unique needs and preferences. It's not about reaching perfection or following rigid guidelines. Instead, it's about embracing a way of eating that brings you closer to your health and wellness goals. As you embark on this carnivore adventure, keep an open mind, be patient with yourself, and enjoy the process of discovering what works best for your body.

# The Science Behind the Diet

The Carnivore Diet, often viewed through a lens of skepticism, is underpinned by a robust scientific framework that challenges the conventional dietary pyramid. At its core, this diet draws on the evolutionary premise that early humans thrived on a predominantly meat-based diet. Modern research into human biology and nutrition provides a compelling argument for the diet's effectiveness, particularly in areas such as weight management, inflammation reduction, and metabolic health.

Firstly, the diet's high protein content plays a crucial role in satiety and weight loss. Proteins are the most satiating macronutrient and can significantly reduce hunger and appetite. This natural appetite control mechanism facilitates a lower caloric intake without the need for meticulous calorie counting or portion control, making weight management more attainable and sustainable.

Moreover, the diet's emphasis on meat—a rich source of bioavailable nutrients—ensures that the body receives essential vitamins and minerals in forms that it can easily absorb and utilize. For instance, meat is a prime source of Vitamin B12, iron, zinc, and selenium, nutrients critical for energy production, immune function, and overall health. The bioavailability of these nutrients from animal sources far exceeds that from plant sources, addressing common nutritional deficiencies and bolstering health.

The Carnivore Diet also has implications for managing inflammation and autoimmune conditions. Many anecdotal reports and emerging studies suggest that eliminating plant-based foods, which can contain anti-nutrients and irritants such as lectins, gluten, and phytates, may reduce systemic inflammation. This reduction in inflammation can alleviate symptoms associated with autoimmune diseases, joint pain, and skin conditions, offering a new lease on life for many.

From a metabolic perspective, the diet's low carbohydrate content can stabilize blood sugar levels and improve insulin sensitivity, making it a potentially effective strategy for managing diabetes and metabolic syndrome. Your body goes into a state of ketosis when you cut back on carbohydrates, burning fat for energy instead of glucose. Weight loss, increased energy, and mental clarity can result from this.

Critically, it's essential to acknowledge the importance of meat quality in this diet. Opting for grass-fed, pasture-raised, and organic meat sources can enhance the diet's nutritional profile, including higher levels of omega-3 fatty acids, which are known for their anti-inflammatory properties.

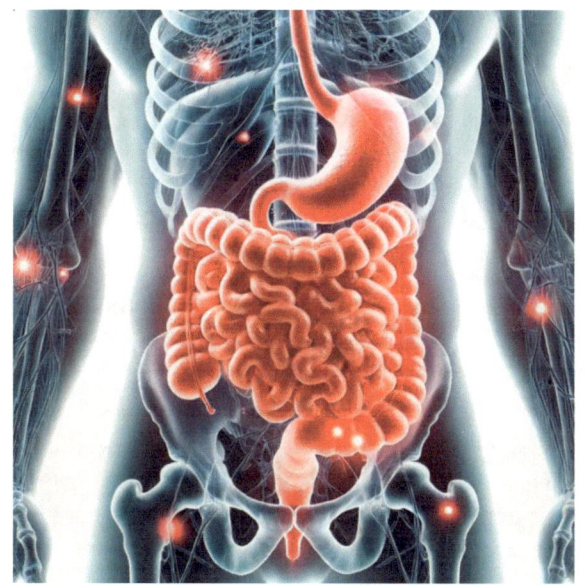

In conclusion, the science behind the Carnivore Diet offers a compelling narrative that aligns with human evolutionary biology and modern nutritional science. By focusing on high-quality, nutrient-dense animal foods, this diet presents a viable alternative to conventional dietary models, promising significant health benefits. As with any dietary approach, individual responses may vary, and it's crucial to listen to your body and consult with healthcare professionals to tailor the diet to your specific health needs and goals.

## Transitioning to Carnivore: Tips and Tricks

Transitioning to a carnivore diet can feel like a leap into the unknown, especially when your kitchen routine has been anything but meat-centric. The key to a smooth transition lies in preparation, flexibility, and a dash of creativity. Here are some useful hints and techniques to help you embrace this transition and handle it with ease.

Firstly, start by gradually increasing your meat intake while reducing non-meat items from your meals. This doesn't have to happen overnight. You might begin with making one meal a day fully carnivorous, then two, and so on, until you find yourself comfortably enjoying a meat-only diet. This gradual shift helps your body and palate adjust without feeling overwhelmed.

Investing in quality meat is crucial. Since meat will be the cornerstone of your diet, opting for the best quality you can afford—think grass-fed beef, wild-caught fish, and free-range poultry—can make a significant difference in both taste and nutritional value. These choices not only support your health but also align with a more sustainable and ethical approach to eating.

Understanding how to cook different cuts of meat can transform your carnivore diet experience. Your air fryer will be your best ally here, allowing you to explore various cooking methods with ease. From air-fried chicken wings that are crispy on the outside and tender on the inside to a succulent pork belly with the perfect crackling, mastering your air fryer's settings will enable you to enjoy a variety of textures and flavors.

Meal planning is another valuable strategy. While the carnivore diet simplifies grocery shopping—your list might be significantly shorter than before—it's still helpful to plan your meals. This ensures variety and prevents boredom. Consider dedicating a few hours each week to batch cooking. Preparing several meals in advance not only saves time but also makes it easier to stick to your new eating pattern.

Don't forget to listen to your body. Transitioning to a carnivore diet is a personal journey, and everyone's experience will be unique. Observe your reactions to various foods and make any adjustments. Some individuals thrive on beef and pork, while others may find they feel better including more fish and poultry.

Lastly, stay hydrated and consider supplementing with electrolytes during the initial transition phase. As your body adapts to a lower carb intake, you might experience changes in fluid balance. Ensuring adequate hydration and electrolyte levels can help smooth this process.

Remember, the goal of transitioning to a carnivore diet is not just about what you eliminate but what you gain. Embrace this change as an opportunity to rediscover the joy of eating simple, nourishing foods that fuel your body and mind. With these tips and your air fryer by your side, you're well-equipped to embark on this carnivorous adventure with confidence and gusto.

## Understanding Your Air Fryer

Your air fryer is about to become your most trusted kitchen ally, especially as you navigate the carnivore diet with gusto and flair. This remarkable appliance, while compact, harnesses the power of rapid air technology to cook your meats to perfection, offering a healthier alternative to traditional frying methods without compromising on taste or texture. Here's a primer to get you started and make the most out of this culinary wizard.

First off, let's demystify how an air fryer works. Imagine a miniature convection oven sitting on your countertop, circulating hot air around food at high speed, cooking it quickly and evenly. This method not only reduces cooking times but also uses significantly less oil, making it a boon for those looking to maintain a lean, high-protein diet. The result? Deliciously crispy meat on the outside and tender, juicy goodness on the inside, all with minimal effort.

Before diving into the world of air-fried carnivorous delights, familiarize yourself with the basic components of your air fryer: the basket and the drawer, which you'll fill with your choice cuts of meat; the temperature control, which allows you to adjust how hot the air circulating around your food gets; and the timer, which helps you track cooking times to avoid over or undercooking your meals. Understanding these elements is crucial for mastering air-fried meats that are nothing short of spectacular.

Now, onto the practical side of things. Start with something simple, like steak or chicken wings, to get a feel for how your air fryer operates. Remember, not all air fryers are created equal; cooking times and temperatures can vary between models, so it's wise to begin with the manufacturer's recommendations and adjust from there based on your preferences. A pro tip: always preheat your air fryer for a few minutes before adding your meat. This guarantees that your food will begin frying right away and will have an enticingly crispy finish.

One of the joys of using an air fryer is the minimal cleanup involved. Thanks to the non-stick surfaces of most baskets and drawers, a quick wash with soapy water is often all that's needed. However, for those times when you're cooking something particularly greasy, a piece of parchment paper or a foil at the bottom of the basket can be a lifesaver, catching drips and keeping your air fryer pristine.

Experimentation is key to unlocking the full potential of your air fryer. Don't be afraid to try different meats, from succulent pork chops to exotic game like bison or elk. Each type of meat will bring its unique flavor and texture to the table, and your air fryer is the perfect tool to explore these culinary adventures. Keep a log of your cooking experiments—note the cut of meat, cooking temperature, and time—to refine your techniques and achieve consistent results that will impress even the most discerning carnivore.

In essence, your air fryer is more than just an appliance; it's your passport to a world of quick, healthy, and incredibly tasty meat-based meals. As you become more comfortable and creative with your air frying, you'll discover that this method of cooking is not only convenient but also transformative, elevating the humblest of meats to gourmet levels. So go ahead, give your carnivore diet the edge it deserves with the power and precision of air frying.

## The Importance of Meat Quality and Selection

Selecting the right quality of meat is not just about taste—it's a critical component of the carnivore diet that impacts your overall health and the success of your dietary goals. With meat being the centerpiece of every meal, understanding how to choose the best quality is paramount. This means looking beyond just the price tag or the appearance of the meat in the grocery store.

First off, let's talk about grass-fed versus grain-fed meat. Grass-fed meat comes from animals that have grazed in pasture their whole lives, as opposed to grain-fed animals that are often raised in confined spaces and fed a diet that includes grains. Why does this matter? Grass-fed meat is higher in key nutrients, including omega-3 fatty acids, which are known for their anti-inflammatory properties, and vitamins A and E. These nutritional benefits can significantly enhance the health benefits of a carnivore diet, from improving heart health to reducing inflammation.

Another important factor is the method of raising the animals. Organic, pasture-raised, and free-range meats are not only more ethical choices but also tend to be healthier. These meats are more likely to come from animals that have lived in better conditions, reducing the risk of harmful bacteria and increasing the nutritional value of the meat. They are also less likely to contain antibiotics or hormones, substances often used in conventional meat production that can have negative effects on human health.

When it comes to selecting seafood, wild-caught is the way to go. Similar to the grass-fed versus grain-fed debate, wild-caught fish have a more natural diet and environment, leading to a better nutritional profile. They tend to be higher in omega-3 fatty acids and lower in pollutants than their farm-raised counterparts.

But how do you navigate this in a practical sense, especially when juggling a busy lifestyle? Start by identifying a reputable butcher or fishmonger in your area, or look for certifications on packaging that indicate higher welfare standards, such as "grass-fed," "organic," or "wild-caught." The cost of these solutions may be higher, but the investment in your health justifies it. Remember, this diet is about subtraction rather than addition, focusing on the quality of what you consume rather than the quantity.

Incorporating a variety of meats into your diet is also crucial. Each type of meat—beef, poultry, fish, lamb, bison, etc.—brings its unique set of nutrients. Rotating your meat selection can help ensure you're getting a broad spectrum of vitamins, minerals, and fats essential for optimal health. This variety also keeps your meals exciting and flavorful, an important aspect of maintaining any dietary lifestyle.

Lastly, don't overlook the importance of how the meat is processed. Select cuts that are as near to their original state as you can. Processed meats, such as sausages or bacon, can contain additives and preservatives that may not align with your health goals. If you do choose processed meats, look for options with minimal ingredients, all of which you can pronounce and recognize.

In summary, the quality and selection of meat on a carnivore diet are foundational to achieving the health benefits and culinary satisfaction this lifestyle promises. By choosing grass-fed, organic, and wild-caught meats and incorporating a variety of meat types into your diet, you're not only enhancing the flavor of your meals but also investing in your long-term health and well-being. With these principles in mind, you're well-equipped to navigate the carnivore diet with confidence, ensuring that each meal brings you one step closer to your health objectives.

# Chapter 2: Quick-Start Breakfasts

Mornings can be a rush, a blur of activity as you juggle getting ready for work, perhaps getting kids off to school, and trying to start your day on a healthy note. The beauty of the carnivore diet, especially when paired with the convenience of an air fryer, is that it simplifies your morning routine without compromising on nutrition or taste. Quick-start breakfasts are all about high-protein, satisfying meals that fuel your body and mind for the day ahead, all ready in minutes with minimal cleanup. Let's dive into how you can revolutionize your mornings with these carnivore diet air fryer recipes.

## Air-Fried Bacon Strips

**Ingredients:**

• 8 thick-cut slices of bacon

**Directions:**

1. Preheat the air fryer to 360°F (182°C).

2. Place the bacon slices in the air fryer basket in a single layer. You may need to cut them in half if your air fryer is small.

3. Cook for 10 minutes, or until the bacon is crispy to your liking. Halfway through cooking, flip the bacon slices for even crispiness.

4. After taking the bacon out of the air fryer, set it on a platter covered with paper towels to remove any extra fat.

**Number of servings:** 4

**Preparation time:** 5 minutes

**Cooking time:** 10 minutes

**Nutritional value per serving:** Calories: 250, Carbs: 0g, Fiber: 0g, Sugars: 0g, Protein: 17g, Saturated fat: 8g, Unsaturated fat: 10g

**Difficulty rating:** ★☆☆☆☆

**Tips for ingredient variations:** Try different types of bacon, such as applewood-smoked or honey-cured, for varying flavors.

## Sausage and Egg Muffins

**Number of servings:** 4

**Preparation time:** 10 minutes

**Cooking time:** 15 minutes

**Nutritional value per serving:** Calories: 320, Carbs: 1g, Fiber: 0g, Sugars: 1g, Protein: 22g, Saturated fat: 10g, Unsaturated fat: 5g

**Difficulty rating:** ★★☆☆☆

**Tips for ingredient variations:** Add chopped vegetables such as bell peppers or onions to the egg mixture for added flavor and nutrition.

**Directions:**

1. Preheat the air fryer to 350°F (177°C).

2. Place the sausage patties in the air fryer basket and cook for 10 minutes, flipping halfway through.

3. In a bowl, crack the eggs and whisk them with salt and pepper.

4. Remove the sausage patties from the air fryer and place them in silicone muffin cups.

5. Pour the whisked eggs over the sausage patties, filling each muffin cup about three-quarters full.

6. Return the muffin cups to the air fryer and cook for an additional 5 minutes, or until the eggs are set.

7. Before serving, carefully take the muffin cups out of the air fryer and let them to cool for one minute.

**Ingredients:**

• 8 sausage patties

• 8 eggs

• Salt and pepper, to taste

## Steak and Eggs

**Ingredients:**

• 2 ribeye steaks (about 1-inch thick)

• 4 eggs

• Salt and pepper, to taste

• 1 tablespoon olive oil

**Directions:**

1. Preheat the air fryer to 400°F (204°C).

2. Season the ribeye steaks with salt and pepper, then brush both sides with olive oil.

3. After putting the steaks in the air fryer basket, cook them for ten minutes, turning them halfway through, for medium-rare.

4. Remove the steaks and let them rest for 5 minutes.

5. While the steaks are resting, crack the eggs into the air fryer basket, seasoned with salt and pepper.

6. Cook the eggs at 370°F (188°C) for 3-4 minutes, or until they are cooked to your liking.

7. Serve the steaks with the air-fried eggs on top or on the side.

**Number of servings:** 2

**Preparation time:** 5 minutes

**Cooking time:** 15 minutes

**Nutritional value per serving:** Calories: 520, Carbs: 0g, Fiber: 0g, Sugars: 0g, Protein: 48g, Saturated fat: 14g, Unsaturated fat: 22g

**Difficulty rating:** ★★★☆☆

**Tips for ingredient variations:** For an extra kick, sprinkle some dried herbs or a pinch of smoked paprika on the steaks before cooking.

## Pork Belly Bites

**Number of servings:** 4

**Preparation time:** 10 minutes

**Cooking time:** 20 minutes

**Nutritional value per serving:** Calories: 507, Carbs: 0g, Fiber: 0g, Sugars: 0g, Protein: 11g, Saturated fat: 17g, Unsaturated fat: 9g

**Difficulty rating:** ★★☆☆☆

**Tips for ingredient variations:** For a spicy kick, add 1/2 tsp of cayenne pepper to the seasoning mix.

**Directions:**

1. Preheat your air fryer to 400°F.

2. Using a bowl, mix the pork belly cubes to coat them equally, season with salt, black pepper, smoked paprika, and garlic powder.

3. Arrange the pork belly cubes in the air fryer basket so that they are not in contact with one another.

4. Cook for 20 minutes, shaking the basket halfway through the cooking time, until the pork belly bites are crispy and golden brown.

5. Remove from the air fryer and let them rest for 2 minutes before serving.

**Ingredients:**

• 1 lb pork belly, cut into 1-inch cubes

• 1 tsp salt

• 1 tsp black pepper

• 1 tsp smoked paprika

• 1/2 tsp garlic powder

## Chicken Liver Pâté on Toast

**Ingredients:**

- 1 lb chicken livers, cleaned
- 2 tbsp unsalted butter
- 1 small onion, finely chopped
- 2 cloves garlic, minced
- 1/4 cup heavy cream
- 1 tsp fresh thyme leaves
- Salt and pepper to taste
- 4 slices of carnivore-friendly bread, toasted

**Directions:**

1. Preheat your air fryer to 370°F.

2. In a skillet over medium heat, melt 1 tbsp of butter. Add the onion and garlic, cooking until soft and translucent, about 3 minutes.

3. Add the chicken livers to the skillet and cook for about 5 minutes, or until they are browned on the outside but still have some pink within.

4. Transfer the chicken liver mixture to a food processor, adding the heavy cream, remaining butter, thyme, salt, and pepper. Blend until smooth.

5. Spread the chicken liver pâté on the toasted slices of bread.

6. Optional: Quickly air fry the prepared toasts for 2 minutes at 370°F for a crispy finish.

**Number of servings:** 4

**Preparation time:** 15 minutes

**Cooking time:** 10 minutes

**Nutritional value per serving:** Calories: 295, Carbs: 5g, Fiber: 0g, Sugars: 1g, Protein: 19g, Saturated fat: 10g, Unsaturated fat: 5g

**Difficulty rating:** ★★★☆☆

**Tips for ingredient variations:** Substitute thyme with rosemary or sage for a different flavor profile.

---

## Crispy Chicken Thighs

**Number of servings:** 4

**Preparation time:** 5 minutes

**Cooking time:** 25 minutes

**Nutritional value per serving:** Calories: 280, Carbs: 0g, Fiber: 0g, Sugars: 0g, Protein: 22g, Saturated fat: 8g, Unsaturated fat: 10g

**Difficulty rating:** ★★☆☆☆

**Tips for ingredient variations:** For a smoky flavor, add 1/4 tsp of smoked paprika to the seasoning mix.

**Directions:**

1. Preheat your air fryer to 380°F.

2. Using paper towels, pat dry the chicken thighs. Each thigh should be seasoned on both sides with paprika, black pepper, garlic powder, and salt.

3. In the air fryer basket, place the chicken thighs skin-side down, making sure they do not touch.

4. Cook for 25 minutes, flipping halfway through the cooking time, until the skin is crispy and the chicken reaches an internal temperature of 165°F.

5. Remove from the air fryer and let them rest for 3 minutes before serving.

**Ingredients:**

- 4 chicken thighs, bone-in, skin-on
- 1 tsp salt
- 1 tsp garlic powder
- 1/2 tsp black pepper
- 1/2 tsp paprika

## Beef Hash

**Ingredients:**

- 1 lb ground beef
- 2 medium russet potatoes, peeled and diced
- 1 small onion, diced
- 1 teaspoon salt
- 1/2 teaspoon black pepper
- 1/2 teaspoon paprika
- 1/4 teaspoon garlic powder

**Directions:**

1. Preheat the air fryer to 400°F.

2. In a large bowl, mix together the ground beef, diced potatoes, onion, salt, pepper, paprika, and garlic powder until well combined.

3. Transfer the beef and potato mixture to the air fryer basket. Spread it out evenly.

4. Cook for 10 minutes. Shake the basket or stir the mixture, then cook for an additional 10 minutes or until the potatoes are crispy and the beef is fully cooked.

5. Serve hot.

**Number of servings:** 4

**Preparation time:** 10 minutes

**Cooking time:** 20 minutes

**Nutritional value per serving:** Calories: 330, Carbs: 20g, Fiber: 2g, Sugars: 1g, Protein: 23g, Saturated fat: 9g, Unsaturated fat: 10g

**Difficulty rating:** ★★☆☆☆

**Tips for ingredient variations:** Feel free to add bell peppers or swap the russet potatoes with sweet potatoes for a different flavor profile.

---

## Spicy Ground Beef and Eggs

**Number of servings:** 4

**Preparation time:** 5 minutes

**Cooking time:** 15 minutes

**Nutritional value per serving:** Calories: 300, Carbs: 1g, Fiber: 0g, Sugars: 0g, Protein: 28g, Saturated fat: 11g, Unsaturated fat: 13g

**Difficulty rating:** ★★★☆☆

**Tips for ingredient variations:** Add diced onions or jalapeños to the beef mixture for an extra kick.

**Directions:**

1. Preheat the air fryer to 370°F.

2. In a bowl, mix the ground beef with chili powder, cumin, salt, black pepper, and cayenne pepper (if using) until well combined.

3. Form the beef mixture into four patties and place them in the air fryer basket.

4. Cook for 10 minutes, flipping halfway through.

5. Crack an egg over each patty. Cook for an additional 5 minutes or until the eggs are cooked to your liking.

6. Serve immediately.

**Ingredients:**

- 1 lb ground beef
- 4 large eggs
- 1 teaspoon chili powder
- 1/2 teaspoon cumin
- 1/2 teaspoon salt
- 1/4 teaspoon black pepper
- 1/4 teaspoon cayenne pepper (optional for extra heat)

## Salmon Patties

**Ingredients:**

- 1 lb canned salmon, drained and flaked
- 1 large egg, beaten
- 2 tablespoons almond flour
- 1 tablespoon mayonnaise
- 1 teaspoon Dijon mustard
- 1/2 teaspoon garlic powder
- 1/2 teaspoon onion powder
- 1/4 teaspoon salt
- 1/4 teaspoon black pepper
- 1 tablespoon fresh dill, chopped (optional)

**Directions:**

1. In a large bowl, combine the salmon, egg, almond flour, mayonnaise, Dijon mustard, garlic powder, onion powder, salt, pepper, and dill (if using). Mix well.

2. Form the mixture into 4 equal-sized patties.

3. Preheat the air fryer to 400°F.

4. Place the salmon patties in the air fryer basket. Cook for 5 minutes, then flip the patties and cook for another 5 minutes, or until golden and crispy.

5. Accompany hot with your preferred side dish.

**Number of servings:** 4

**Preparation time:** 15 minutes

**Cooking time:** 10 minutes

**Nutritional value per serving:** Calories: 250, Carbs: 2g, Fiber: 0.5g, Sugars: 0g, Protein: 27g, Saturated fat: 3g, Unsaturated fat: 5g

**Difficulty rating:** ★★★☆☆

**Tips for ingredient variations:** Substitute almond flour with coconut flour for a different taste or add chopped capers for an extra burst of flavor.

---

## Duck Breast with Crispy Skin

**Number of servings:** 2

**Preparation time:** 10 minutes

**Cooking time:** 25 minutes

**Nutritional value per serving:** Calories: 375, Carbs: 0g, Fiber: 0g, Sugars: 0g, Protein: 45g, Saturated fat: 5g, Unsaturated fat: 10g

**Difficulty rating:** ★★★☆☆

**Tips for ingredient variations:** For an Asian twist, marinate the duck with soy sauce, ginger, and garlic before air frying.

**Directions:**

1. Preheat the air fryer to 360°F (182°C).

2. Duck breasts should have their skin scored in a diamond pattern without slicing through to the meat. Use thyme, salt, and pepper to season both sides.

3. Place the duck breasts skin side up in the air fryer basket. Cook for 25 minutes, or until the skin is crispy and the meat reaches an internal temperature of 165°F (74°C).

4. Let the duck rest for 5 minutes before slicing.

**Ingredients:**

- 2 duck breasts, skin on
- Salt and pepper, to taste
- 1 tsp thyme, dried

## Lamb Chops with Rosemary

**Ingredients:**

- 4 lamb chops
- 2 tbsp olive oil
- 2 tsp rosemary, dried
- Salt and pepper, to taste

**Directions:**

1. Preheat the air fryer to 400°F (204°C).

2. Rub both sides of the lamb chops with olive oil and season with rosemary, salt, and pepper.

3. Make sure the lamb chops in the air fryer basket are not in contact with one another. Cook for 15 minutes, flipping halfway through, or until they reach an internal temperature of 145°F (63°C) for medium-rare.

4. Let the lamb chops rest for 3 minutes before serving.

**Number of servings:** 2

**Preparation time:** 5 minutes

**Cooking time:** 15 minutes

**Nutritional value per serving:** Calories: 310, Carbs: 0g, Fiber: 0g, Sugars: 0g, Protein: 30g, Saturated fat: 9g, Unsaturated fat: 5g

**Difficulty rating:** ★★☆☆☆

**Tips for ingredient variations:** Substitute rosemary with mint for a classic flavor pairing or add garlic for an extra kick.

## Turkey Bacon Wraps

**Number of servings:** 4

**Preparation time:** 10 minutes

**Cooking time:** 10 minutes

**Nutritional value per serving:** Calories: 150, Carbs: 1g, Fiber: 0g, Sugars: 0g, Protein: 20g, Saturated fat: 2g, Unsaturated fat: 3g

**Difficulty rating:** ★★☆☆☆

**Tips for ingredient variations:** For a spicy kick, mix chili powder into the seasoning.

**Directions:**

1. Preheat the air fryer to 390°F (199°C).

2. Season the chicken tenders with salt, pepper, paprika, and garlic powder.

3. Wrap each chicken tender with two slices of turkey bacon, securing with toothpicks if necessary.

4. Place the wrapped chicken tenders in the air fryer basket and cook for 10 minutes, or until the chicken is cooked through and the bacon is crispy.

5. Remove toothpicks before serving.

**Ingredients:**

- 8 slices of turkey bacon
- 4 chicken tenders, seasoned with salt and pepper
- 1 tsp paprika
- 1 tsp garlic powder

## *Pork Loin Slices*

**Ingredients:**

- 1 lb pork loin, sliced into 1/2-inch thick pieces
- 1 tsp salt
- 1/2 tsp black pepper
- 1 tsp garlic powder
- 1 tsp onion powder
- 1/2 tsp smoked paprika

**Directions:**

1. Preheat the air fryer to 400°F.

2. Season the pork loin slices evenly with salt, pepper, garlic powder, onion powder, and smoked paprika.

3. Make sure the seasoned pork slices do not overlap when you arrange them in the air fryer basket in a single layer.

4. Cook for 10 minutes, then flip the slices and cook for an additional 10 minutes or until the pork reaches an internal temperature of 145°F.

5. Take out of the air fryer, then give it a three-minute rest before serving.

**Number of servings:** 4

**Preparation time:** 10 minutes

**Cooking time:** 20 minutes

**Nutritional value per serving:** Calories: 190, Carbs: 1g, Fiber: 0g, Sugars: 0g, Protein: 29g, Saturated fat: 2g, Unsaturated fat: 3g

**Difficulty rating:** ★★☆☆☆

**Tips for ingredient variations:** For a spicier kick, add 1/4 tsp of cayenne pepper to the seasoning mix.

---

## *Bison Breakfast Sausage*

**Number of servings:** 4

**Preparation time:** 15 minutes

**Cooking time:** 15 minutes

**Nutritional value per serving:** Calories: 152, Carbs: 0g, Fiber: 0g, Sugars: 0g, Protein: 22g, Saturated fat: 3g, Unsaturated fat: 2g

**Difficulty rating:** ★★★☆☆

**Tips for ingredient variations:** For a sweeter sausage, add 1 tsp of maple syrup to the bison mixture before forming patties.

**Directions:**

1. In a large bowl, combine the ground bison with sage, thyme, nutmeg, cayenne pepper, salt, and black pepper. Mix well.

2. Create eight tiny patties out of the mixture.

3. Preheat the air fryer to 375°F.

4. Place the patties in the air fryer basket, ensuring they are not touching.

5. Cook for 15 minutes, flipping halfway through, or until the internal temperature reaches 160°F.

6. Serve immediately.

**Ingredients:**

- 1 lb ground bison
- 1 tsp sage
- 1/2 tsp thyme
- 1/4 tsp nutmeg
- 1/4 tsp cayenne pepper
- 1/2 tsp salt
- 1/4 tsp black pepper

## Venison Steaks

**Ingredients:**

• 2 venison steaks (about 6 oz each)

• 1 tsp salt

• 1/2 tsp black pepper

• 1 tsp rosemary, finely chopped

• 1 tbsp olive oil

**Directions:**

1. Preheat the air fryer to 400°F.

2. Rub each venison steak with olive oil, then season with salt, pepper, and rosemary.

3. Place the steaks in the air fryer basket, ensuring they do not overlap.

4. Cook for 6 minutes; flip the steaks and continue cooking for an additional 6 minutes to achieve a medium-rare doneness, or cook until your desired doneness is reached.

5. Let the steaks rest for 5 minutes before serving.

**Number of servings:** 2

**Preparation time:** 5 minutes

**Cooking time:** 12 minutes

**Nutritional value per serving:** Calories: 275, Carbs: 0g, Fiber: 0g, Sugars: 0g, Protein: 38g, Saturated fat: 3g, Unsaturated fat: 5g

**Difficulty rating:** ★★★☆☆

**Tips for ingredient variations:** For a more robust flavor, marinate the venison steaks in a mixture of olive oil, balsamic vinegar, and minced garlic for at least 2 hours before cooking.

## Elk Meatballs

**Number of servings:** 4

**Preparation time:** 15 minutes

**Cooking time:** 20 minutes

**Nutritional value per serving:** Calories: 250, Carbs: 3g, Fiber: 1g, Sugars: 0g, Protein: 35g, Saturated fat: 4g, Unsaturated fat: 3g

**Difficulty rating:** ★★☆☆☆

**Tips for ingredient variations:** For a spicier kick, add 1/4 tsp of red pepper flakes to the meat mixture.

**Directions:**

1. In a large bowl, combine the ground elk meat, beaten egg, almond flour, minced garlic, salt, black pepper, dried oregano, and smoked paprika. Blend thoroughly until all components are dispersed equally.

2. Preheat the air fryer to 400°F.

3. Shape the ingredients into meatballs with a diameter of about one inch.

4. Place the meatballs in the air fryer basket, ensuring they are not touching.

5. Cook for 10 minutes, then flip the meatballs and cook for an additional 10 minutes, or until the meatballs are browned and cooked through.

**Ingredients:**

• 1 lb ground elk meat

• 1 egg, beaten

• 1/4 cup almond flour

• 2 cloves garlic, minced

• 1 tsp salt

• 1/2 tsp black pepper

• 1/2 tsp dried oregano

• 1/4 tsp smoked paprika

## Rabbit Tenderloin

**Ingredients:**

- 2 rabbit tenderloins
- 1 tbsp olive oil
- 1 tsp rosemary, finely chopped
- 1/2 tsp salt
- 1/4 tsp black pepper
- 1/4 tsp garlic powder

**Directions:**

1. Preheat the air fryer to 390°F.

2. Rub the rabbit tenderloins with olive oil, then season with rosemary, salt, black pepper, and garlic powder.

3. Place the seasoned tenderloins in the air fryer basket.

4. Bake for fifteen minutes, or until the rabbit is thoroughly cooked and has taken on a hint of color on the outside.

5. Let rest for 5 minutes before slicing.

**Number of servings:** 2

**Preparation time:** 10 minutes

**Cooking time:** 15 minutes

**Nutritional value per serving:** Calories: 220, Carbs: 0g, Fiber: 0g, Sugars: 0g, Protein: 30g, Saturated fat: 1g, Unsaturated fat: 2g

**Difficulty rating:** ★★★☆☆

**Tips for ingredient variations:** Thyme or marjoram can be used in place of rosemary for a different flavor profile.

## Goose Breast Jerky

**Number of servings:** 4

**Preparation time:** 8 hours (includes marinating time)

**Cooking time:** 4 hours

**Nutritional value per serving:** Calories: 180, Carbs: 3g, Fiber: 0g, Sugars: 1g, Protein: 25g, Saturated fat: 0.5g, Unsaturated fat: 1g

**Difficulty rating:** ★★★★☆

**Tips for ingredient variations:** For a sweeter jerky, add 1 tbsp of honey or maple syrup to the marinade.

**Directions:**

1. In a bowl, combine soy sauce, Worcestershire sauce, apple cider vinegar, smoked paprika, garlic powder, onion powder, black pepper, and cayenne pepper (if using) to create the marinade.

2. Ensure that every piece of thinly sliced goose breast is fully coated by adding it to the marinade. Cover and refrigerate for at least 8 hours, or overnight.

3. Preheat the air fryer to 180°F.

4. Remove the goose slices from the marinade and place them in the air fryer basket in a single layer, ensuring they do not overlap.

5. Cook until the jerky is chewy and dry, about 4 hours.

6. Let the jerky cool before storing in an airtight container.

**Ingredients:**

- 1 lb goose breast, thinly sliced
- 1/2 cup soy sauce (or coconut aminos for a soy-free option)
- 1/4 cup Worcestershire sauce
- 2 tbsp apple cider vinegar
- 1 tbsp smoked paprika
- 1 tsp garlic powder
- 1 tsp onion powder
- 1/2 tsp black pepper
- 1/4 tsp cayenne pepper (optional)

## Quail Eggs in Nest

**Ingredients:**

• 12 quail eggs

• 1 cup of shredded parmesan cheese

• ½ teaspoon of black pepper

• ½ teaspoon of salt

**Directions:**

1. Preheat the air fryer to 375°F (190°C).

2. In a bowl, mix the shredded parmesan cheese with salt and pepper.

3. Take a tablespoon of the cheese mixture and place it in the air fryer basket, flattening it slightly to form a nest shape. Repeat with the remaining cheese, ensuring some space between each nest.

4. Air fry the cheese nests for about 6 minutes or until they start to turn golden.

5. Crack a quail egg into each cheese nest carefully.

6. Return the basket to the air fryer and cook for an additional 6-8 minutes, or until the eggs are cooked to your liking.

7. Carefully remove the nests from the basket and serve immediately.

**Number of servings:** 2

**Preparation time:** 10 minutes

**Cooking time:** 15 minutes

**Nutritional value per serving:** Calories: 210, Carbs: 1g, Fiber: 0g, Sugars: 0g, Protein: 18g, Saturated fat: 8g, Unsaturated fat: 4g

**Difficulty rating:** ★★☆☆☆

**Tips for ingredient variations:** For a spicy kick, sprinkle some red pepper flakes on top of the nests before adding the eggs.

## Lamb Liver with Onions

**Number of servings:** 4

**Preparation time:** 10 minutes

**Cooking time:** 12 minutes

**Nutritional value per serving:** Calories: 220, Carbs: 10g, Fiber: 2g, Sugars: 4g, Protein: 25g, Saturated fat: 2g, Unsaturated fat: 5g

**Difficulty rating:** ★★★☆☆

**Tips for ingredient variations:** For a hint of sweetness, add a tablespoon of balsamic vinegar to the onions before cooking.

**Directions:**

1. Preheat the air fryer to 370°F (188°C).

2. In a large bowl, toss the lamb liver slices with olive oil, salt, pepper, and thyme until evenly coated.

3. Spread the seasoned liver slices in the air fryer basket in a single layer. Depending on how big your air fryer is, you might have to cook in batches.

4. Air fry for 6 minutes, then add the sliced onions over the liver.

5. Continue to air fry for an additional 6 minutes or until the liver is cooked through and the onions are tender and slightly caramelized.

6. Serve the lamb liver hot, topped with the cooked onions.

**Ingredients:**

• 1 lb lamb liver, thinly sliced

• 2 large onions, thinly sliced

• 2 tablespoons olive oil

• 1 teaspoon salt

• ½ teaspoon ground black pepper

• 1 teaspoon dried thyme

## Beef Kidney Pie

**Ingredients:**

- 1 lb beef kidney, cleaned and diced
- 1 cup beef broth
- ½ cup diced carrots
- ½ cup frozen peas
- 1 onion, diced
- 2 cloves garlic, minced
- 1 teaspoon Worcestershire sauce
- 1 teaspoon salt
- ½ teaspoon black pepper
- 1 tablespoon cornstarch
- 1 tablespoon water
- 1 pre-made pie crust, cut into 6 rounds to fit air fryer basket

**Directions:**

1. Preheat the air fryer to 350°F (177°C).

2. Add the beef kidney, onion, and garlic to a skillet over medium heat and cook, seasoning with salt and pepper, until the kidney is browned and the onions are tender.

3. Add the carrots, peas, beef broth, and Worcestershire sauce to the skillet. Simmer for 10 minutes.

4. In a small bowl, make a slurry by mixing cornstarch and water. Stir into the kidney mixture to thicken the sauce.

5. Place the pie crust rounds in the air fryer basket, gently pressing them into the shape of the basket.

6. Spoon the kidney mixture into each crust, filling them up to the top.

7. Air fry for 15 minutes or until the pie crusts are golden and crispy.

8. Before serving, allow it cool for a few minutes.

**Number of servings:** 6

**Preparation time:** 20 minutes

**Cooking time:** 25 minutes

**Nutritional value per serving:** Calories: 320, Carbs: 22g, Fiber: 2g, Sugars: 3g, Protein: 26g, Saturated fat: 6g, Unsaturated fat: 4g

**Difficulty rating:** ★★★★☆

**Tips for ingredient variations:** Substitute beef kidney with lamb kidney for a milder flavor, or add mushrooms for an earthy taste.

---

## Pork Riblets

**Number of servings:** 4

**Preparation time:** 10 minutes

**Cooking time:** 20 minutes

**Nutritional value per serving:** Calories: 310, Carbs: 1g, Fiber: 0g, Sugars: 0g, Protein: 25g, Saturated fat: 6g, Unsaturated fat: 5g

**Difficulty rating:** ★★☆☆☆

**Tips for ingredient variations:** Feel free to experiment with different spices or herbs to match your taste preferences. For a sweeter version, you can add a touch of honey or maple syrup to the spice mix.

**Directions:**

1. Preheat your air fryer to 400°F (200°C).

2. In a small bowl, mix together salt, black pepper, garlic powder, smoked paprika, and cayenne pepper.

3. Rub the spice mixture all over the pork riblets, ensuring they are well coated.

4. Place the riblets in the air fryer basket, making sure they are not overcrowded.

5. Cook for 10 minutes, then flip the riblets and cook for an additional 10 minutes or until they are crispy on the outside and tender on the inside.

6. Remove from the air fryer and let them rest for 5 minutes before serving.

**Ingredients:**

- 2 lbs pork riblets
- 1 tbsp salt
- 1 tsp black pepper
- 2 tsp garlic powder
- 1 tsp smoked paprika
- 1/2 tsp cayenne pepper (optional for extra heat)

## Chicken Heart Skewers

**Ingredients:**

- 1 lb chicken hearts, cleaned and trimmed
- 2 tbsp olive oil
- 1 tbsp soy sauce
- 1 tsp garlic powder
- 1 tsp onion powder
- 1/2 tsp chili flakes
- Salt and pepper to taste
- Water-soaked wooden skewers, soaking for half an hour

**Directions:**

1. In a bowl, whisk together olive oil, soy sauce, garlic powder, onion powder, chili flakes, salt, and pepper.

2. Add the chicken hearts to the marinade and stir to coat evenly. Cover and refrigerate for at least 1 hour, or overnight for best flavor.

3. Preheat your air fryer to 375°F (190°C).

4. Thread the marinated chicken hearts onto the soaked skewers.

5. Place the skewers in the air fryer basket, ensuring they do not touch each other.

6. Cook for 5 minutes, then flip the skewers and cook for another 5 minutes or until the chicken hearts are fully cooked.

7. Serve immediately.

**Number of servings:** 4

**Preparation time:** 15 minutes (plus marinating time)

**Cooking time:** 10 minutes

**Nutritional value per serving:** Calories: 180, Carbs: 1g, Fiber: 0g, Sugars: 0g, Protein: 26g, Saturated fat: 3g, Unsaturated fat: 5g

**Difficulty rating:** ★★★☆☆

**Tips for ingredient variations:** Marinate the chicken hearts in different international flavors like teriyaki, peri-peri, or a Greek-style marinade for variety.

## Duck Fat Fried Eggs

**Number of servings:** 2

**Preparation time:** 5 minutes

**Cooking time:** 8 minutes

**Nutritional value per serving:** Calories: 237, Carbs: 1g, Fiber: 0g, Sugars: 0g, Protein: 13g, Saturated fat: 5g, Unsaturated fat: 7g

**Difficulty rating:** ★☆☆☆☆

**Tips for ingredient variations:** For an extra flavor boost, sprinkle some fresh herbs like chives or parsley over the eggs just before serving.

**Directions:**

1. Preheat your air fryer to 350°F (175°C).

2. Place the duck fat in the air fryer basket and let it melt for about 1 minute.

3. Crack the eggs into the air fryer basket, being careful not to break the yolks.

4. Season with salt and pepper.

5. Cook for 6-8 minutes, or until the eggs are cooked to your desired doneness.

6. Carefully remove the eggs from the air fryer and serve immediately.

**Ingredients:**

- 4 large eggs
- 2 tbsp duck fat
- Salt and pepper to taste

# Chapter 3: Satisfying Lunches

Lunchtime is your midday recharge, a crucial moment to fuel your body with nutrient-dense, satisfying meals that keep you energized and focused for the rest of the day. The Carnivore Diet, with its emphasis on high-quality animal products, provides an excellent framework for crafting lunches that are not only delicious but deeply nourishing. Utilizing the air fryer for these meals adds a layer of convenience and texture that transforms even the simplest of ingredients into a culinary delight. Let's explore how to make the most of your midday meal with quick, protein-rich lunches that cater to your busy lifestyle while adhering to the carnivore ethos.

With these air fryer recipes, you'll enjoy delicious, protein-rich lunches that keep you energized and satisfied, proving that eating well on the Carnivore Diet is not only possible but truly enjoyable.

## Beef Rib Roast

**Ingredients:**

- 1 (4 lb) beef rib roast
- 2 tbsp coarse sea salt
- 1 tbsp black pepper
- 2 tsp garlic powder
- 1 tsp onion powder
- 1 tsp dried rosemary

**Directions:**

1. Preheat the air fryer to 390°F (200°C).

2. In a small bowl, mix together the sea salt, black pepper, garlic powder, onion powder, and dried rosemary.

3. Make sure the beef rib roast is uniformly coated by rubbing it with the spice mixture.

4. Place the roast in the air fryer basket, fat side up.

5. Cook for 60 minutes, or until the roast reaches an internal temperature of 135°F (57°C) for medium-rare. Adjust cooking time for desired doneness.

6. Remove the roast from the air fryer and let it rest for 10 minutes before slicing.

**Number of servings:** 6

**Preparation time:** 10 minutes

**Cooking time:** 60 minutes

**Nutritional value per serving:** Calories: 590, Carbs: 1g, Fiber: 0g, Sugars: 0g, Protein: 50g, Saturated fat: 24g, Unsaturated fat: 27g

**Difficulty rating:** ★★★☆☆

**Tips for ingredient variations:** For a smoky flavor, add 1 tsp of smoked paprika to the spice mixture.

## Lamb Shoulder Chops

**Number of servings:** 4

**Preparation time:** 5 minutes

**Cooking time:** 20 minutes

**Nutritional value per serving:** Calories: 330, Carbs: 0g, Fiber: 0g, Sugars: 0g, Protein: 34g, Saturated fat: 9g, Unsaturated fat: 6g

**Difficulty rating:** ★★☆☆☆

**Tips for ingredient variations:** Substitute rosemary with thyme or oregano for a different herb flavor.

**Directions:**

1. Preheat the air fryer to 400°F (204°C).

2. In a small bowl, mix together the olive oil, rosemary, and minced garlic.

3. Sprinkle salt and pepper on both sides of the lamb chops.

4. Rub the olive oil mixture onto both sides of each chop.

5. Place the chops in the air fryer basket, ensuring they are not touching.

6. Cook for 10 minutes, then flip the chops and cook for an additional 10 minutes, or until they reach an internal temperature of 145°F (63°C) for medium-rare.

7. Remove the chops from the air fryer and let them rest for 3 minutes before serving.

**Ingredients:**

- 4 lamb shoulder chops (about 1 inch thick)
- 2 tbsp olive oil
- 1 tbsp fresh rosemary, finely chopped
- 2 cloves garlic, minced
- Salt and pepper, to taste

## *Pulled Pork*

**Ingredients:**

• 3 lbs pork shoulder, cut into 2-inch chunks

• 1 tbsp salt

• 2 tsp black pepper

• 1 tsp smoked paprika

• 1 tsp garlic powder

• 1 tsp onion powder

• 1/2 cup barbecue sauce (for serving)

**Directions:**

1. Preheat the air fryer to 350°F (177°C).

2. In a large bowl, mix together the salt, black pepper, smoked paprika, garlic powder, and onion powder.

3. Toss the pork shoulder chunks in the spice mixture until they are well coated.

4. Place the pork chunks in the air fryer basket, ensuring they are not overcrowded.

5. Simmer the pork for ninety minutes, or until it is quite soft and readily shredded with a fork. Depending on the size of your air fryer, cooking may need to be done in batches.

6. Remove the pork from the air fryer and let it cool slightly before shredding with two forks.

7. Serve the pulled pork with barbecue sauce on the side or mixed in.

**Number of servings:** 8

**Preparation time:** 15 minutes

**Cooking time:** 90 minutes

**Nutritional value per serving:** Calories: 310, Carbs: 7g, Fiber: 0g, Sugars: 5g, Protein: 44g, Saturated fat: 5g, Unsaturated fat: 6g

**Difficulty rating:** ★★★☆☆

**Tips for ingredient variations:** For a spicier version, add 1 tsp of chili powder or cayenne pepper to the spice mixture.

## *Crispy Chicken Wings*

**Number of servings:** 4

**Preparation time:** 10 minutes

**Cooking time:** 22 minutes

**Nutritional value per serving:** Calories: 310, Carbs: 1g, Fiber: 0g, Sugars: 0g, Protein: 24g, Saturated fat: 6g, Unsaturated fat: 9g

**Difficulty rating:** ★★☆☆☆

**Tips for ingredient variations:** For a spicy kick, add 1/4 tsp of cayenne pepper to the seasoning mix.

**Directions:**

1. Combine the paprika, garlic powder, black pepper, baking powder, and salt in a big basin.

2. Add the chicken wings in the bowl and toss to coat them in the spice mixture evenly.

3. Preheat the air fryer to 380°F (193°C).

4. Arrange the wings in a single layer in the air fryer basket, ensuring they are not touching for optimal air flow.

5. Cook the wings for 22 minutes, turning them over halfway through, or until they are crispy and golden brown.

6. Present right away with your preferred dipping sauce.

**Ingredients:**

• 2 lbs chicken wings, patted dry

• 1 tbsp baking powder

• 1 tsp salt

• 1/2 tsp black pepper

• 1/2 tsp garlic powder

• 1/2 tsp paprika

# Turkey Legs

**Ingredients:**

- 4 turkey legs
- 2 tbsp olive oil
- 1 tsp salt
- 1 tsp smoked paprika
- 1/2 tsp ground black pepper
- 1/2 tsp dried thyme

**Directions:**

1. Rub each turkey leg with olive oil, then season with salt, smoked paprika, ground black pepper, and dried thyme.

2. Preheat the air fryer to 350°F (177°C).

3. Place the turkey legs in the air fryer basket, ensuring they are not touching.

4. Cook for 60 minutes, flipping the legs halfway through the cooking time, until the skin is crispy and the meat is fully cooked.

5. Let the turkey legs rest for 5 minutes before serving.

**Number of servings:** 4

**Preparation time:** 5 minutes

**Cooking time:** 60 minutes

**Nutritional value per serving:** Calories: 475, Carbs: 0g, Fiber: 0g, Sugars: 0g, Protein: 64g, Saturated fat: 8g, Unsaturated fat: 5g

**Difficulty rating:** ★★★☆☆

**Tips for ingredient variations:** For a herby flavor, add 1/2 tsp of rosemary or sage to the seasoning mix.

# Bison Burgers

**Number of servings:** 4

**Preparation time:** 15 minutes

**Cooking time:** 10 minutes

**Nutritional value per serving (without cheese):** Calories: 240, Carbs: 0g, Fiber: 0g, Sugars: 0g, Protein: 22g, Saturated fat: 9g, Unsaturated fat: 10g

**Difficulty rating:** ★★☆☆☆

**Tips for ingredient variations:** For added flavor, mix minced onions or jalapeños into the bison mixture before forming patties.

**Directions:**

1. In a bowl, mix the ground bison with salt, black pepper, and garlic powder until well combined.

2. Form the mixture into 4 equal-sized patties.

3. Preheat the air fryer to 370°F (188°C).

4. Place the bison patties in the air fryer basket, ensuring they are not touching.

5. Cook for 10 minutes, flipping halfway through, for medium doneness.

6. If you're using cheese, melt a slice on top of each patty in the final minute of cooking.

7. Serve the bison burgers immediately.

**Ingredients:**

- 1 lb ground bison
- 1 tsp salt
- 1/2 tsp black pepper
- 1/2 tsp garlic powder
- 4 slices of carnivore-approved cheese (optional)

## *Venison Roast*

**Ingredients:**

- 2 lbs venison roast
- 1 tbsp olive oil
- 2 tsp salt
- 1 tsp black pepper
- 1 tsp garlic powder
- 1 tsp onion powder
- 1 tsp dried thyme

**Directions:**

1. Preheat the air fryer to 390°F (199°C).

2. Rub the venison roast evenly with olive oil.

3. Combine the salt, black pepper, onion, garlic, and dried thyme powders in a small bowl. Sprinkle the seasoning mix over the venison roast, ensuring it is fully coated.

4. Place the seasoned venison roast in the air fryer basket.

5. Cook for 60 minutes, or until the venison reaches an internal temperature of 145°F (63°C) for medium-rare.

6. Remove the venison roast from the air fryer and let it rest for 10 minutes before slicing.

**Number of servings:** 4

**Preparation time:** 15 minutes

**Cooking time:** 60 minutes

**Nutritional value per serving:** Calories: 375, Carbs: 0g, Fiber: 0g, Sugars: 0g, Protein: 52g, Saturated fat: 3g, Unsaturated fat: 2g

**Difficulty rating:** ★★★☆☆

**Tips for ingredient variations:** For a more robust flavor, marinate the venison in red wine and rosemary overnight before cooking.

## *Elk Loin*

**Number of servings:** 2

**Preparation time:** 10 minutes

**Cooking time:** 15 minutes

**Nutritional value per serving:** Calories: 310, Carbs: 0g, Fiber: 0g, Sugars: 0g, Protein: 45g, Saturated fat: 4g, Unsaturated fat: 3g

**Difficulty rating:** ★★★☆☆

**Tips for ingredient variations:** Add a sprig of rosemary or thyme to the air fryer basket for an aromatic twist.

**Directions:**

1. Preheat the air fryer to 400°F (204°C).

2. Rub the elk loin with olive oil.

3. Combine sea salt, cracked black pepper, smoked paprika, and garlic powder in a bowl. Sprinkle the seasoning mix over the elk loin, ensuring it is evenly coated.

4. Place the seasoned elk loin in the air fryer basket.

5. Cook for 15 minutes, flipping halfway through, or until the elk loin reaches an internal temperature of 135°F (57°C) for medium-rare.

6. Let the elk loin rest for 5 minutes before slicing.

**Ingredients:**

- 1 lb elk loin
- 1 tbsp olive oil
- 1 tsp sea salt
- 1/2 tsp cracked black pepper
- 1/2 tsp smoked paprika
- 1/4 tsp garlic powder

## Rabbit Stew

### Ingredients:

- 2 lbs rabbit, cut into pieces
- 1 tbsp olive oil
- 1 large onion, chopped
- 2 cloves garlic, minced
- 2 carrots, sliced
- 2 cups beef broth
- 1 cup red wine
- 1 tsp salt
- 1/2 tsp black pepper
- 1/2 tsp dried thyme
- 2 bay leaves

### Directions:

1. If your air fryer has a slow cook function, set it to 300°F (149°C). If not, preheat to the lowest setting.

2. Heat the olive oil in a large skillet over medium heat. After adding, brown the rabbit pieces on all sides. Transfer to the air fryer basket.

3. In the same skillet, add the onion and garlic, cooking until soft. Add the carrots and cook for an additional 2 minutes. Transfer the mixture to the air fryer basket over the rabbit.

4. Pour beef broth and red wine over the rabbit and vegetables. Season with salt, pepper, thyme, and add bay leaves.

5. Cook in the air fryer on slow cook mode for 4 hours, or until the rabbit is tender and the stew has thickened. If using a standard air fryer, cook at the lowest setting for as long as possible, checking and stirring occasionally.

6. Remove bay leaves before serving.

**Number of servings:** 4

**Preparation time:** 20 minutes

**Cooking time:** 4 hours (slow cook mode if available)

**Nutritional value per serving:** Calories: 345, Carbs: 8g, Fiber: 1g, Sugars: 3g, Protein: 50g, Saturated fat: 1g, Unsaturated fat: 3g

**Difficulty rating:** ★★★★☆

**Tips for ingredient variations:** For a heartier stew, add chopped potatoes or mushrooms during the last hour of cooking.

## Goose Carnitas

**Number of servings:** 4

**Preparation time:** 20 minutes

**Cooking time:** 4 hours

**Nutritional value per serving:** Calories: 310, Carbs: 5g, Fiber: 1g, Sugars: 2g, Protein: 44g, Saturated fat: 3g, Unsaturated fat: 5g

**Difficulty rating:** ★★★★☆

**Tips for ingredient variations:** For a spicier version, add 1 tsp of chili powder or a diced chipotle pepper in adobo sauce to the seasoning mix.

### Directions:

1. In a large bowl, mix together salt, black pepper, ground cumin, dried oregano, and minced garlic. When the geese pieces are well covered with the spice mixture, add them to the bowl and toss again.

2. Place the seasoned goose pieces into the air fryer basket.

3. In a small bowl, combine the orange juice, lime juice, and chicken broth. Pour this mixture over the goose in the air fryer.

4. Cook at 250°F for 4 hours, or until the goose meat is tender and easily shreds with a fork.

5. Use two forks to shred the goose meat inside the air fryer basket, then increase the temperature to 400°F and cook for an additional 5-10 minutes to crisp up the edges.

6. Serve the goose carnitas with your choice of sides or use it as a filling for tacos or burritos.

### Ingredients:

- 2 lbs goose breast, cut into 2-inch pieces
- 1 tbsp salt
- 2 tsp black pepper
- 1 tbsp ground cumin
- 2 tsp dried oregano
- 4 cloves garlic, minced
- 1 orange, juiced
- 1 lime, juiced
- 1/2 cup chicken broth

## Quail in Air Fryer

**Ingredients:**

- 4 quail, cleaned and patted dry
- 2 tbsp olive oil
- 1 tsp salt
- 1/2 tsp black pepper
- 1 tsp thyme, dried
- 1 tsp rosemary, dried

**Directions:**

1. Preheat the air fryer to 390°F.

2. Rub each quail with olive oil, then season with salt, black pepper, thyme, and rosemary.

3. Place the quail in the air fryer basket, ensuring they are not touching.

4. Cook for 15 minutes, or until the quail are golden brown and cooked through, flipping halfway through the cooking time.

5. Let the quail rest for 5 minutes before serving.

**Number of servings:** 2

**Preparation time:** 10 minutes

**Cooking time:** 15 minutes

**Nutritional value per serving:** Calories: 290, Carbs: 0g, Fiber: 0g, Sugars: 0g, Protein: 25g, Saturated fat: 5g, Unsaturated fat: 7g

**Difficulty rating:** ★★★☆☆

**Tips for ingredient variations:** For a citrus twist, add a tablespoon of lemon zest to the seasoning mix before rubbing it on the quail.

---

## Lamb Gyros

**Number of servings:** 4

**Preparation time:** 15 minutes

**Cooking time:** 20 minutes

**Nutritional value per serving (excluding optional toppings):** Calories: 320, Carbs: 1g, Fiber: 0g, Sugars: 0g, Protein: 22g, Saturated fat: 10g, Unsaturated fat: 7g

**Difficulty rating:** ★★★☆☆

**Tips for ingredient variations:** For a different flavor profile, substitute ground lamb with ground beef or turkey. Add fresh herbs like mint or parsley to the lamb mixture for a fresh twist.

**Directions:**

1. In a large bowl, combine ground lamb, garlic powder, onion powder, salt, black pepper, dried oregano, cumin, and smoked paprika. Thoroughly mix until all the spices are dispersed throughout the meat.

2. Using the lamb mixture, form it into a loaf that fits in the basket of your air fryer.

3. Preheat the air fryer to 360°F.

4. Place the lamb loaf in the air fryer basket and cook for 20 minutes, or until the internal temperature reaches 160°F.

5. Remove the lamb from the air fryer and let it rest for 5 minutes before slicing thinly.

6. Serve the lamb slices on low-carb tortillas or lettuce wraps, topped with optional sliced onions, diced tomatoes, and tzatziki sauce.

**Ingredients:**

- 1 lb ground lamb
- 2 tsp garlic powder
- 2 tsp onion powder
- 1 tsp salt
- 1 tsp black pepper
- 2 tsp dried oregano
- 1 tsp cumin
- 1/2 tsp smoked paprika
- 4 low-carb tortillas or lettuce wraps (for serving)
- Optional toppings: sliced onions, diced tomatoes, tzatziki sauce

## Beef Brisket

**Ingredients:**

- 3 lbs beef brisket
- 2 tbsp coarse salt
- 1 tbsp black pepper
- 1 tbsp smoked paprika
- 2 tsp garlic powder
- 1 tsp onion powder
- 1/2 cup beef broth

**Directions:**

1. Combine the onion, garlic, and smoked paprika powders, black pepper, and salt in a small bowl.

2. Rub the spice mixture all over the beef brisket, ensuring it's fully coated.

3. Pour beef broth into the bottom of the air fryer basket.

4. Place the seasoned brisket in the air fryer basket.

5. Set the air fryer to 300°F and cook for 4 hours, or until the brisket is tender and easily pulls apart with a fork.

6. Let the brisket rest for 10 minutes before slicing against the grain.

**Number of servings:** 6

**Preparation time:** 15 minutes

**Cooking time:** 4 hours

**Nutritional value per serving:** Calories: 470, Carbs: 1g, Fiber: 0g, Sugars: 0g, Protein: 76g, Saturated fat: 15g, Unsaturated fat: 20g

**Difficulty rating:** ★★★☆☆

**Tips for ingredient variations:** For a sweeter flavor, add 1 tbsp of brown sugar to the spice mix. For a spicier brisket, include 1 tsp of cayenne pepper.

## Pork Cheek Tacos

**Number of servings:** 4

**Preparation time:** 20 minutes

**Cooking time:** 3 hours

**Nutritional value per serving:** Calories: 310, Carbs: 15g, Fiber: 2g, Sugars: 4g, Protein: 44g, Saturated fat: 6g, Unsaturated fat: 8g

**Difficulty rating:** ★★★★☆

**Tips for ingredient variations:** For a tangier flavor, add a tablespoon of apple cider vinegar to the orange and lime juice mixture.

**Directions:**

1. In a small bowl, mix together chili powder, cumin, salt, black pepper, and cayenne pepper.

2. Rub the spice mixture all over the pork cheeks.

3. Place the seasoned pork cheeks in the air fryer basket. Distribute the finely chopped onion and minced garlic on top.

4. Mix orange juice and lime juice together and pour over the pork cheeks.

5. Set the air fryer to 300°F and cook for 3 hours, or until the pork cheeks are tender and easily shredded with a fork.

6. Shred the pork cheeks and serve on corn tortillas. Garnish with fresh cilantro, diced onions, and lime wedges.

**Ingredients:**

- 2 lbs pork cheeks, trimmed
- 1 tbsp chili powder
- 1 tsp cumin
- 1 tsp salt
- 1/2 tsp black pepper
- 1/4 tsp cayenne pepper
- 1 onion, finely chopped
- 2 cloves garlic, minced
- 1/2 cup orange juice
- 1/4 cup lime juice
- Corn tortillas, for serving
- Fresh cilantro, diced onions, and lime wedges for garnish

## Chicken Drumsticks

**Ingredients:**

• 8 chicken drumsticks

• 1 tbsp olive oil

• 1 tsp salt

• 1/2 tsp black pepper

• 1 tsp garlic powder

• 1 tsp paprika

• 1/2 tsp dried thyme

**Directions:**

1. Using paper towels, pat the chicken drumsticks dry.

2. In a large bowl, mix together olive oil, salt, black pepper, garlic powder, paprika, and dried thyme.

3. After adding the chicken drumsticks to the bowl, toss them around to ensure the spice mixture coats them evenly.

4. Place the drumsticks in the air fryer basket, ensuring they are not touching.

5. Set the air fryer to 380°F and cook for 25 minutes, turning the drumsticks halfway through the cooking time, until they are crispy on the outside and cooked through.

6. Serve hot.

**Number of servings:** 4

**Preparation time:** 10 minutes

**Cooking time:** 25 minutes

**Nutritional value per serving:** Calories: 290, Carbs: 1g, Fiber: 0g, Sugars: 0g, Protein: 27g, Saturated fat: 4g, Unsaturated fat: 5g

**Difficulty rating:** ★★☆☆

**Tips for ingredient variations:** For a smoky flavor, substitute paprika with smoked paprika. Add 1/4 tsp of cayenne pepper to the spice mixture for added spiciness

## Duck Confit

**Number of servings:** 4

**Preparation time:** 15 minutes (plus overnight marinating)

**Cooking time:** 4 hours

**Nutritional value per serving:** Calories: 1100, Carbs: 1g, Fiber: 0g, Sugars: 1g, Protein: 31g, Saturated fat: 23g, Unsaturated fat: 25g

**Difficulty rating:** ★★★★☆

**Tips for ingredient variations:** For added flavor, include orange zest or star anise to the duck fat before cooking.

**Directions:**

1. Mix salt, sugar, and black pepper in a bowl. Coat the duck legs in the mixture. Put the duck legs, bay leaves, and thyme in a shallow dish. Cover and refrigerate overnight.

2. Preheat the air fryer to 200°F (93°C). To get rid of the salt combination, rinse the duck legs under cold water and pat dry with paper towels.

3. Pour melted duck fat over the duck legs in the air fryer basket, making sure they are well submerged.

4. Cook for 4 hours, or until the meat is tender and pulls away from the bone easily.

5. Remove the duck legs from the fat and let them cool. For a crispy skin, increase the air fryer temperature to 400°F (204°C) and cook for an additional 5 minutes.

**Ingredients:**

• 4 duck legs with thighs

• 4 tbsp salt

• 2 tbsp sugar

• 1 tbsp black pepper

• 4 garlic cloves, smashed

• 4 sprigs of thyme

• 2 bay leaves, crushed

• 4 cups duck fat, melted

## Liver and Onions

**Ingredients:**

- 1 lb beef liver, thinly sliced
- 2 large onions, sliced
- 1/4 cup flour (for coating)
- 1 tsp salt
- 1/2 tsp black pepper
- 4 tbsp butter

**Directions:**

1. Preheat the air fryer to 370°F (188°C).

2. After carefully dusting each liver slice with flour and shaking off any excess, season each slice with salt and pepper.

3. Melt butter in the air fryer for 1 minute. Add the liver and onions to the air fryer basket.

4. Cook for 7 minutes, then stir the onions and flip the liver slices. Cook for an additional 7-8 minutes, or until the liver is cooked through and onions are caramelized.

5. Serve the liver topped with the onions.

**Number of servings:** 4

**Preparation time:** 10 minutes

**Cooking time:** 15 minutes

**Nutritional value per serving:** Calories: 310, Carbs: 15g, Fiber: 1g, Sugars: 2g, Protein: 27g, Saturated fat: 8g, Unsaturated fat: 3g

**Difficulty rating:** ★★☆☆☆

**Tips for ingredient variations:** For a gluten-free version, use almond flour or coconut flour instead of regular flour for coating the liver.

## Kidney Beanless Chili

**Number of servings:** 4

**Preparation time:** 10 minutes

**Cooking time:** 20 minutes

**Nutritional value per serving:** Calories: 480, Carbs: 13g, Fiber: 3g, Sugars: 8g, Protein: 34g, Saturated fat: 15g, Unsaturated fat: 17g

**Difficulty rating:** ★★☆☆☆

**Tips for ingredient variations:** For a spicier chili, add diced jalapeños or increase the amount of chili powder.

**Directions:**

1. Preheat the air fryer to 370°F (188°C).

2. In a bowl, mix together the ground beef, onion, garlic, chili powder, cumin, salt, pepper, and smoked paprika.

3. Spoon the beef mixture into the air fryer basket; heat for 10 minutes, stirring occasionally, until the meat is cooked through.

4. Stir together the diced tomatoes and tomato paste in the basket.

5. Cook for an additional 10 minutes, or until the chili thickens.

6. Serve hot, with optional toppings like sour cream or shredded cheese if you'd like.

**Ingredients:**

- 2 lbs ground beef
- 1 large onion, diced
- 2 cloves garlic, minced
- 2 tbsp chili powder
- 1 tbsp cumin
- 1 tsp salt
- 1/2 tsp black pepper
- 1/2 tsp smoked paprika
- 1 can (14 oz) diced tomatoes, undrained
- 1 can (6 oz) tomato paste

## Ribeye Steak

**Ingredients:**

• 2 ribeye steaks (about 1-inch thick)

• 1 tbsp olive oil

• Salt and pepper, to taste

**Directions:**

1. Preheat the air fryer to 400°F (204°C).

2. After liberally seasoning each steak with salt and pepper, rub it with olive oil.

3. Place the steaks in the air fryer basket, ensuring they do not overlap.

4. Cook for 6 minutes, then turn the steaks over and cook for a further 6 minutes to achieve a medium-rare doneness, or cook until your desired doneness is reached.

5. Let the steaks rest for 5 minutes before serving to allow the juices to redistribute.

**Number of servings:** 2

**Preparation time:** 5 minutes

**Cooking time:** 12 minutes

**Nutritional value per serving:** Calories: 540, Carbs: 0g, Fiber: 0g, Sugars: 0g, Protein: 46g, Saturated fat: 14g, Unsaturated fat: 25g

**Difficulty rating:** ★★★☆☆

**Tips for ingredient variations:** For a herby flavor, add a sprinkle of dried rosemary or thyme before cooking.

## Salmon Fillets

**Number of servings:** 2

**Preparation time:** 5 minutes

**Cooking time:** 10 minutes

**Nutritional value per serving:** Calories: 345, Carbs: 0g, Fiber: 0g, Sugars: 0g, Protein: 34g, Saturated fat: 5g, Unsaturated fat: 15g

**Difficulty rating:** ★★☆☆☆

**Tips for ingredient variations:** For a spicy kick, add a pinch of cayenne pepper to the seasoning mix before cooking.

**Directions:**

1. Preheat the air fryer to 400°F (204°C).

2. Brush each salmon fillet with olive oil and season with garlic powder, dill, salt, and pepper.

3. Place the salmon fillets in the air fryer basket, skin-side down.

4. Cook for 10 minutes, or until the salmon easily flakes with a fork.

5. Serve immediately with lemon wedges on the side.

**Ingredients:**

• 2 salmon fillets (6 oz each)

• 1 tbsp olive oil

• 1 tsp garlic powder

• 1 tsp dried dill

• Salt and pepper, to taste

• Lemon wedges, for serving

## Trout Almondine

**Ingredients:**

- 2 trout fillets (about 6 oz each)
- 1 tbsp almond flour
- 2 tbsp sliced almonds
- 1 tbsp butter, melted
- 1 tsp lemon zest
- Salt and pepper, to taste
- Lemon wedges, for serving

**Directions:**

1. Preheat the air fryer to 370°F (187°C).

2. Season the trout fillets with salt and pepper. Sprinkle almond flour evenly over the fillets.

3. In a small bowl, mix together the sliced almonds, melted butter, and lemon zest.

4. Top each fillet with the almond mixture.

5. Place the trout fillets in the air fryer basket, ensuring they do not overlap.

6. Simmer for 12 minutes, or until the almonds are golden brown and the trout is thoroughly cooked.

7. Serve immediately with lemon wedges on the side.

**Number of servings:** 2

**Preparation time:** 10 minutes

**Cooking time:** 12 minutes

**Nutritional value per serving:** Calories: 295, Carbs: 2g, Fiber: 1g, Sugars: 0g, Protein: 31g, Saturated fat: 7g, Unsaturated fat: 10g

**Difficulty rating:** ★★★☆☆

**Tips for ingredient variations:** For an extra nutty flavor, substitute almond flour with finely ground hazelnuts.

## Shark Steaks

**Number of servings:** 2

**Preparation time:** 10 minutes

**Cooking time:** 12 minutes

**Nutritional value per serving:** Calories: 280, Carbs: 0g, Fiber: 0g, Sugars: 0g, Protein: 40g, Saturated fat: 1g, Unsaturated fat: 3g

**Difficulty rating:** ★★★☆☆

**Tips for ingredient variations:** For a herby flavor, add a sprinkle of dried dill or thyme to the seasoning mix.

**Directions:**

1. Preheat the air fryer to 400°F.

2. Rub each shark steak with olive oil, then season with lemon zest, salt, pepper, and garlic powder.

3. Place the steaks in the air fryer basket, ensuring they do not overlap.

4. Cook for 6 minutes, then flip the steaks and cook for an additional 6 minutes, or until the steaks are cooked through and slightly golden on the outside.

5. Let the steaks rest for 5 minutes before serving.

**Ingredients:**

- 2 shark steaks (about 6 oz each)
- 1 tbsp olive oil
- 1 tsp lemon zest
- Salt and pepper, to taste
- 1/2 tsp garlic powder

## Swordfish Skewers

**Ingredients:**

• 1 lb swordfish, cut into 1-inch cubes

• 2 tbsp olive oil

• 1 tbsp lemon juice

• 1 tsp paprika

• 1/2 tsp cumin

• Salt and pepper, to taste

• Water-soaked wooden skewers, soaking for half an hour

**Directions:**

1. In a bowl, whisk together olive oil, lemon juice, paprika, cumin, salt, and pepper.

2. Add the swordfish cubes to the marinade and stir to coat evenly. Give it a cover and chill for a minimum of half an hour.

3. Preheat your air fryer to 400°F.

4. Thread the marinated swordfish cubes onto the soaked skewers.

5. Place the skewers in the air fryer basket, ensuring they do not touch each other.

6. Cook for 5 minutes, then flip the skewers and cook for another 5 minutes, or until the swordfish is fully cooked and slightly charred on the edges.

7. Serve immediately.

**Number of servings:** 4

**Preparation time:** 15 minutes (plus 30 minutes for marinating)

**Cooking time:** 10 minutes

**Nutritional value per serving:** Calories: 220, Carbs: 1g, Fiber: 0g, Sugars: 0g, Protein: 25g, Saturated fat: 2g, Unsaturated fat: 5g

**Difficulty rating:** ★★★☆☆

**Tips for ingredient variations:** For a Mediterranean twist, add chopped olives and capers to the marinade.

---

## Tuna Steaks

**Number of servings:** 2

**Preparation time:** 5 minutes

**Cooking time:** 8 minutes

**Nutritional value per serving:** Calories: 300, Carbs: 1g, Fiber: 0g, Sugars: 0g, Protein: 45g, Saturated fat: 1g, Unsaturated fat: 4g

**Difficulty rating:** ★★☆☆☆

**Tips for ingredient variations:** For a spicy kick, add a pinch of red pepper flakes to the soy sauce mixture.

**Directions:**

1. Preheat the air fryer to 400°F.

2. In a small bowl, mix together soy sauce, olive oil, ground ginger, salt, and pepper.

3. Apply the mixture to the tuna steaks on both sides.

4. Place the tuna steaks in the air fryer basket, ensuring they do not overlap.

5. Cook for 4 minutes, then flip the steaks and cook for an additional 4 minutes for medium-rare, or adjust the cooking time to your preferred doneness.

6. Sprinkle sesame seeds over the steaks before serving.

**Ingredients:**

• 2 tuna steaks (about 6 oz each)

• 1 tbsp soy sauce

• 1 tbsp olive oil

• 1/2 tsp ground ginger

• Salt and pepper, to taste

• Sesame seeds, for garnish

# Chapter 4: Hearty Dinners

Hearty Dinners are the cornerstone of a satisfying day, especially when following a carnivore diet. These meals are not just about ending the day on a high note; they're about providing your body with the essential nutrients it needs to repair, recover, and prepare for the challenges ahead. With the air fryer, creating these nutrient-dense, protein-packed dinners becomes not only effortless but also a delightful culinary adventure. Let's delve into some dinner recipes that will make your carnivore heart sing with joy and satisfaction.

Each of these dinner recipes showcases the versatility and convenience of the air fryer in creating meals that adhere to the carnivore diet. They prove that following a meat-centric diet doesn't mean sacrificing variety or flavor. On the contrary, it opens up a world of culinary possibilities, allowing you to enjoy hearty, nutritious dinners that support your health goals. So, embrace the simplicity and power of air frying to transform your evening meals into something truly special.

## Prime Rib

**Ingredients:**

- 1 (5 lb) prime rib roast
- 2 tbsp coarse sea salt
- 1 tbsp freshly ground black pepper
- 2 tsp dried rosemary
- 2 tsp garlic powder
- 1 tsp onion powder
- 1/2 cup beef broth

**Directions:**

1. Preheat the air fryer to 390°F (200°C).

2. In a small bowl, mix together sea salt, black pepper, dried rosemary, garlic powder, and onion powder.

3. Rub the spice mixture all over the prime rib roast, ensuring it is evenly coated.

4. Place the roast in the air fryer basket, fat side up.

5. Cook for 90 minutes, or until the roast reaches an internal temperature of 135°F (57°C) for medium-rare. Adjust cooking time for desired doneness.

6. Remove the roast from the air fryer and let it rest for 10 minutes before slicing.

7. Serve with a side of beef broth for dipping.

**Number of servings:** 6

**Preparation time:** 10 minutes

**Cooking time:** 90 minutes

**Nutritional value per serving:** Calories: 890, Carbs: 1g, Fiber: 0g, Sugars: 0g, Protein: 88g, Saturated fat: 40g, Unsaturated fat: 38g

**Difficulty rating:** ★★★☆☆

**Tips for ingredient variations:** For a smoky flavor, add 1 tsp of smoked paprika to the spice mixture.

## Lamb Rack

**Number of servings:** 4

**Preparation time:** 15 minutes

**Cooking time:** 22 minutes

**Nutritional value per serving:** Calories: 410, Carbs: 1g, Fiber: 0g, Sugars: 0g, Protein: 45g, Saturated fat: 17g, Unsaturated fat: 18g

**Difficulty rating:** ★★★☆☆

**Tips for ingredient variations:** For an herbaceous twist, add 1 tbsp of chopped fresh rosemary to the olive oil mixture.

**Directions:**

1. Preheat the air fryer to 400°F (204°C).

2. In a small bowl, mix together olive oil, kosher salt, black pepper, dried thyme, minced garlic, and Dijon mustard.

3. Rub the mixture evenly over the rack of lamb.

4. Place the lamb rack in the air fryer basket, meat side facing up.

5. Cook for 22 minutes, or until the lamb reaches an internal temperature of 145°F (63°C) for medium-rare.

6. Remove the lamb rack from the air fryer and let it rest for 5 minutes before carving between the ribs.

7. Serve immediately.

**Ingredients:**

- 1 (2 lb) rack of lamb, trimmed
- 2 tbsp olive oil
- 2 tsp kosher salt
- 1 tsp black pepper
- 1 tsp dried thyme
- 2 cloves garlic, minced
- 1 tsp Dijon mustard

## Carnivore Meatloaf

**Ingredients:**

- 2 lbs ground beef
- 2 eggs
- 1 tsp salt
- 1/2 tsp black pepper
- 1 tsp garlic powder
- 1 tsp onion powder

**Directions:**

1. In a large bowl, mix together ground beef, eggs, salt, black pepper, garlic powder, and onion powder until well combined.

2. Using the basket of your air fryer, form the mixture into a loaf shape.

3. Preheat the air fryer to 370°F (188°C).

4. Place the meatloaf in the air fryer basket.

5. Cook for 40 minutes, or until the meatloaf reaches an internal temperature of 160°F (71°C).

6. Take the meatloaf out of the air fryer, then let it five minutes to rest before slicing.

7. Serve hot.

**Number of servings:** 4

**Preparation time:** 15 minutes

**Cooking time:** 40 minutes

**Nutritional value per serving:** Calories: 480, Carbs: 1g, Fiber: 0g, Sugars: 0g, Protein: 56g, Saturated fat: 18g, Unsaturated fat: 20g

**Difficulty rating:** ★★☆☆☆

**Tips for ingredient variations:** For added flavor, mix in 1 tbsp of Worcestershire sauce or hot sauce into the beef mixture before cooking.

## Crispy Skin Duck Breast

**Ingredients:**

- 2 duck breasts, skin on
- Salt and pepper, to taste
- 1 tsp thyme, dried

**Directions:**

1. Preheat the air fryer to 360°F (182°C).

2. Duck breasts should have their skin scored in a diamond pattern without slicing through to the meat. Add salt, pepper, and thyme to both sides of the dish.

3. Place the duck breasts skin side up in the air fryer basket. Cook for 25 minutes, or until the skin is crispy and the meat reaches an internal temperature of 165°F (74°C).

4. Let the duck rest for 5 minutes before slicing.

**Number of servings:** 2

**Preparation time:** 15 minutes

**Cooking time:** 25 minutes

**Nutritional value per serving:** Calories: 375, Carbs: 0g, Fiber: 0g, Sugars: 0g, Protein: 45g, Saturated fat: 5g, Unsaturated fat: 10g

**Difficulty rating:** ★★★☆☆

**Tips for ingredient variations:** For an Asian twist, marinate the duck with soy sauce, ginger, and garlic before air frying.

## Whole Roasted Chicken

**Ingredients:**

- 1 whole chicken (about 4 lbs)
- 2 tbsp olive oil
- 1 tbsp salt
- 1 tsp black pepper
- 2 tsp garlic powder
- 1 tsp paprika
- 1 lemon, halved
- 4 sprigs of thyme

**Directions:**

1. Preheat the air fryer to 360°F (182°C).

2. Rub the whole chicken with olive oil. Combine the paprika, garlic powder, black pepper, and salt in a small bowl. Apply this spice mixture evenly over the chicken.

3. Place the lemon halves and thyme sprigs inside the chicken cavity.

4. Secure the legs with kitchen twine, then tuck the tips of the wings under the torso.

5. Slide the chicken into the air fryer basket, breast side down. Cook for 30 minutes, then flip the chicken and cook for an additional 30 minutes, or until the chicken reaches an internal temperature of 165°F (74°C).

6. Give the chicken ten minutes to rest before slicing.

**Number of servings:** 4

**Preparation time:** 10 minutes

**Cooking time:** 60 minutes

**Nutritional value per serving:** Calories: 422, Carbs: 1g, Fiber: 0g, Sugars: 0g, Protein: 35g, Saturated fat: 9g, Unsaturated fat: 13g

**Difficulty rating:** ★★★☆☆

**Tips for ingredient variations:** For a citrusy flavor, add orange slices to the cavity along with the lemon.

## Pork Belly Porchetta

**Number of servings:** 4

**Preparation time:** 20 minutes

**Cooking time:** 40 minutes

**Nutritional value per serving:** Calories: 580, Carbs: 1g, Fiber: 0g, Sugars: 0g, Protein: 22g, Saturated fat: 22g, Unsaturated fat: 25g

**Difficulty rating:** ★★★★☆

**Tips for ingredient variations:** Add chili flakes to the herb mixture for a spicy kick.

**Directions:**

1. Preheat the air fryer to 390°F (198°C).

2. Crush the garlic, thyme, rosemary, and fennel seeds in a mortar and pestle. Mix in the lemon zest, salt, and pepper.

3. Rub this herb mixture all over the pork belly, ensuring it gets into the scores of the skin.

4. Tightly roll the pork belly and tie with kitchen twine.

5. Place the pork belly roll in the air fryer basket. Cook for 40 minutes, or until the skin is crispy and the meat is tender.

6. Prior to slicing, let the porchetta rest for ten minutes.

**Ingredients:**

- 2 lbs pork belly, skin scored
- 2 tbsp fennel seeds
- 1 tbsp rosemary, chopped
- 2 tsp thyme, chopped
- 4 garlic cloves, minced
- Zest of 1 lemon
- 1 tbsp salt
- 1 tsp black pepper

## Beef Short Ribs

**Ingredients:**

- 2 lbs beef short ribs
- 1 tbsp coarse sea salt
- 1 tsp black pepper
- 1 tsp garlic powder
- 1 tsp onion powder
- 1/2 tsp smoked paprika

**Directions:**

1. Preheat the air fryer to 380°F (193°C).

2. Mix the sea salt, black pepper, garlic powder, onion powder, and smoked paprika in a small bowl.

3. Evenly rub the beef short ribs with the spice mixture.

4. Place the seasoned ribs in the air fryer basket, ensuring they are not overlapping.

5. Cook for 45 minutes, flipping halfway through the cooking time, until the ribs are tender and the outside is crispy.

6. Let the ribs rest for 5 minutes before serving.

**Number of servings:** 4

**Preparation time:** 10 minutes

**Cooking time:** 45 minutes

**Nutritional value per serving:** Calories: 480, Carbs: 1g, Fiber: 0g, Sugars: 0g, Protein: 44g, Saturated fat: 20g, Unsaturated fat: 22g

**Difficulty rating:** ★★★☆☆

**Tips for ingredient variations:** For a sweeter flavor, add a tablespoon of brown sugar to the spice mix. For a spicy kick, include 1 tsp of chili powder.

---

## Venison Backstrap

**Number of servings:** 2

**Preparation time:** 5 minutes

**Cooking time:** 12 minutes

**Nutritional value per serving:** Calories: 320, Carbs: 0g, Fiber: 0g, Sugars: 0g, Protein: 48g, Saturated fat: 3g, Unsaturated fat: 5g

**Difficulty rating:** ★★★☆☆

**Tips for ingredient variations:** For a more robust flavor, marinate the venison in a mixture of balsamic vinegar, olive oil, and minced garlic for at least 2 hours before cooking.

**Directions:**

1. Preheat the air fryer to 400°F (204°C).

2. Rub the venison backstrap with olive oil.

3. Combine sea salt, cracked black pepper, dried rosemary, and garlic powder in a bowl. Sprinkle the seasoning mix over the venison backstrap, ensuring it is evenly coated.

4. Place the seasoned venison backstrap in the air fryer basket.

5. Cook for 6 minutes, then flip the backstrap and cook for an additional 6 minutes for medium-rare, or adjust the cooking time to your preferred doneness.

6. Let the venison backstrap rest for 5 minutes before slicing.

**Ingredients:**

- 1 lb venison backstrap, trimmed
- 2 tbsp olive oil
- 1 tsp sea salt
- 1/2 tsp cracked black pepper
- 1 tsp dried rosemary
- 1/2 tsp garlic powder

## Elk Rib Rack

**Ingredients:**

- 1 elk rib rack (about 2 lbs)
- 2 tbsp olive oil
- 1 tbsp coarse sea salt
- 1 tsp ground black pepper
- 1 tsp dried thyme
- 1/2 tsp garlic powder
- 1/2 tsp onion powder

**Directions:**

1. Preheat the air fryer to 375°F (190°C).

2. Rub the elk rib rack with olive oil.

3. Mix together the sea salt, ground black pepper, dried thyme, garlic powder, and onion powder in a bowl.

4. Evenly coat the elk rib rack with the seasoning mix.

5. Place the seasoned rib rack in the air fryer basket.

6. Cook for 25 minutes, or until the elk ribs reach an internal temperature of 145°F (63°C) for medium-rare.

7. Before slicing the elk rib rack into individual ribs, let it rest for ten minutes.

**Number of servings:** 4

**Preparation time:** 15 minutes

**Cooking time:** 25 minutes

**Nutritional value per serving:** Calories: 310, Carbs: 1g, Fiber: 0g, Sugars: 0g, Protein: 45g, Saturated fat: 4g, Unsaturated fat: 5g

**Difficulty rating:** ★★★★☆

**Tips for ingredient variations:** For a sweeter taste, add a glaze of honey and Dijon mustard in the last 5 minutes of cooking.

## Rabbit Confit

**Number of servings:** 2

**Preparation time:** 20 minutes (plus overnight for seasoning)

**Cooking time:** 4 hours

**Nutritional value per serving:** Calories: 980, Carbs: 1g, Fiber: 0g, Sugars: 0g, Protein: 67g, Saturated fat: 22g, Unsaturated fat: 25g

**Difficulty rating:** ★★★★☆

**Tips for ingredient variations:** Substitute thyme with rosemary or sage for a different herbaceous note.

**Directions:**

1. The night before cooking, rub the rabbit legs with sea salt, black pepper, minced garlic, and thyme. Transfer to a shallow dish, cover, and chill for the nigh

2. Preheat the air fryer to 200°F (93°C).

3. Rinse the rabbit legs under cold water to remove the seasoning. Pat dry with paper towels.

4. Place the rabbit legs in the air fryer basket and pour the melted duck fat over them, ensuring they are completely submerged in fat.

5. Cook for 4 hours, or until the meat is tender and easily pulls off the bone.

6. For a crispy finish, increase the air fryer temperature to 400°F (204°C) and cook for an additional 5 minutes.

**Ingredients:**

- 2 rabbit legs
- 4 tbsp sea salt
- 2 tsp black pepper
- 4 garlic cloves, minced
- 4 sprigs of thyme
- 2 cups of duck fat, melted

## Goose Leg Quarter

**Ingredients:**

- 2 goose leg quarters
- 2 tbsp olive oil
- 1 tbsp sea salt
- 1 tsp ground black pepper
- 2 tsp dried thyme
- 4 garlic cloves, smashed

**Directions:**

1. Preheat the air fryer to 325°F (163°C).

2. Rub the goose leg quarters with olive oil, then season with sea salt, ground black pepper, dried thyme, and garlic cloves.

3. Place the seasoned goose legs in the air fryer basket.

4. Cook for 1 hour and 30 minutes, or until the skin is crispy and the meat is tender and fully cooked.

5. To let the fluids to disperse, let the dish rest for ten minutes before serving.

**Number of servings:** 2

**Preparation time:** 15 minutes

**Cooking time:** 1 hour 30 minutes

**Nutritional value per serving:** Calories: 720, Carbs: 2g, Fiber: 0g, Sugars: 0g, Protein: 98g, Saturated fat: 16g, Unsaturated fat: 18g

**Difficulty rating:** ★★★☆☆

**Tips for ingredient variations:** Add a splash of white wine to the air fryer basket before cooking for an added depth of flavor.

## Quail with Bacon

**Number of servings:** 2

**Preparation time:** 10 minutes

**Cooking time:** 20 minutes

**Nutritional value per serving:** Calories: 540, Carbs: 0g, Fiber: 0g, Sugars: 0g, Protein: 45g, Saturated fat: 12g, Unsaturated fat: 15g

**Difficulty rating:** ★★★☆☆

**Tips for ingredient variations:** For a sweet and savory twist, brush the bacon with maple syrup before wrapping the quail.

**Directions:**

1. Preheat the air fryer to 390°F (198°C).

2. Season the quail with salt, black pepper, and dried rosemary.

3. Wrap each quail with 2 slices of bacon, securing with toothpicks if necessary.

4. Make sure the bacon-wrapped quail are not touching when you place them in the air fryer basket.

5. Cook, turning halfway through, for 20 minutes, or until the quail is cooked through and the bacon is crispy.

6. Remove toothpicks and let rest for 5 minutes before serving.

**Ingredients:**

- 4 quail, cleaned and patted dry
- 8 slices of bacon
- 1 tsp salt
- 1/2 tsp black pepper
- 1 tsp dried rosemary

## Lamb Shank

**Ingredients:**

- 2 lamb shanks
- 1 tbsp olive oil
- 1 tsp salt
- 1/2 tsp black pepper
- 1 tsp rosemary, dried
- 1 tsp thyme, dried
- 2 cloves garlic, minced
- 1 cup beef broth

**Directions:**

1. Preheat the air fryer to 320°F (160°C).

2. Rub the lamb shanks with olive oil, salt, black pepper, rosemary, thyme, and minced garlic.

3. Place the lamb shanks in the air fryer basket.

4. Cook for 30 minutes, then add beef broth to the basket.

5. Lower the heat to 300°F (150°C) and continue cooking the lamb for a further one and a half hours, or until it is fork-tender and easily removes from the bone.

6. Serve the lamb shanks with the juices from the air fryer basket as a sauce.

**Number of servings:** 2

**Preparation time:** 10 minutes

**Cooking time:** 2 hours

**Nutritional value per serving:** Calories: 380, Carbs: 2g, Fiber: 0g, Sugars: 0g, Protein: 48g, Saturated fat: 10g, Unsaturated fat: 8g

**Difficulty rating:** ★★★☆☆

**Tips for ingredient variations:** Add root vegetables like carrots and parsnips around the lamb shanks during the last hour of cooking for a complete meal.

## Beef Cheek Barbacoa

**Number of servings:** 4

**Preparation time:** 20 minutes

**Cooking time:** 4 hours

**Nutritional value per serving:** Calories: 450, Carbs: 5g, Fiber: 1g, Sugars: 2g, Protein: 50g, Saturated fat: 15g, Unsaturated fat: 10g

**Difficulty rating:** ★★★★☆

**Tips for ingredient variations:** For a sweeter barbacoa, add 1/4 cup of orange juice to the liquid mixture.

**Directions:**

1. Preheat the air fryer to 300°F (150°C).

2. Rub the beef cheeks with vegetable oil, salt, and black pepper.

3. In a bowl, mix together apple cider vinegar, minced garlic, chipotle peppers, cumin, oregano, cloves, lime juice, and beef broth.

4. Place the beef cheeks in the air fryer basket and pour the mixture over them.

5. Cook for 4 hours, or until the beef is very tender and shreds easily.

6. Shred the beef cheeks with two forks and serve as desired, such as in tacos or over rice.

**Ingredients:**

- 2 lbs beef cheeks, trimmed
- 1 tbsp vegetable oil
- 2 tsp salt
- 1 tsp black pepper
- 1/2 cup apple cider vinegar
- 4 cloves garlic, minced
- 2 chipotle peppers in adobo sauce, chopped
- 1 tsp ground cumin
- 1 tsp dried oregano
- 1/2 tsp ground cloves
- 1/4 cup lime juice
- 1/4 cup beef broth

## Pork Chops

**Ingredients:**

- 2 pork chops, 1-inch thick
- 1 tbsp olive oil
- 1 tsp garlic powder
- 1 tsp smoked paprika
- Salt and pepper, to taste

**Directions:**

1. Preheat the air fryer to 380°F (193°C).

2. Rub each pork chop with olive oil, then season with garlic powder, smoked paprika, salt, and pepper.

3. Place the pork chops in the air fryer basket, ensuring they do not overlap.

4. Cook for 6 minutes, then flip the pork chops and cook for an additional 6 minutes, or until the internal temperature reaches 145°F (63°C).

5. Let the pork chops rest for 3 minutes before serving.

**Number of servings:** 2

**Preparation time:** 5 minutes

**Cooking time:** 12 minutes

**Nutritional value per serving:** Calories: 290, Carbs: 0g, Fiber: 0g, Sugars: 0g, Protein: 29g, Saturated fat: 5g, Unsaturated fat: 10g

**Difficulty rating:** ★★☆☆☆

**Tips for ingredient variations:** For a herbaceous flavor, add a sprinkle of dried thyme or rosemary to the seasoning mix before cooking.

## Chicken Quarter Legs

**Number of servings:** 4

**Preparation time:** 10 minutes

**Cooking time:** 25 minutes

**Nutritional value per serving:** Calories: 310, Carbs: 0g, Fiber: 0g, Sugars: 0g, Protein: 24g, Saturated fat: 6g, Unsaturated fat: 8g

**Difficulty rating:** ★★☆☆☆

**Tips for ingredient variations:** For a zesty flavor, add a squeeze of lemon juice or zest to the seasoning mix before cooking.

**Directions:**

1. Preheat the air fryer to 380°F (193°C).

2. Rub the chicken quarter legs with olive oil, then season with salt, black pepper, garlic powder, and smoked paprika.

3. Place the chicken legs in the air fryer basket, skin-side up, ensuring they do not touch.

4. Bake for twenty-five minutes, or until the chicken is 165°F (74°C) inside and golden brown.

5. Let rest for 5 minutes before serving.

**Ingredients:**

- 4 chicken quarter legs
- 2 tbsp olive oil
- 1 tsp salt
- 1/2 tsp black pepper
- 1 tsp garlic powder
- 1 tsp smoked paprika

## Duck Legs

**Ingredients:**

- 2 duck legs
- 2 tbsp soy sauce
- 1 tbsp honey
- 1 tsp five-spice powder
- 2 cloves garlic, minced
- 1 inch ginger, grated
- Salt and pepper, to taste

**Directions:**

1. In a bowl, mix together soy sauce, honey, five-spice powder, garlic, ginger, salt, and pepper to create the marinade.

2. Apply the marinade to the duck legs and place them in the fridge to marinate for at least two hours, but preferably overnight.

3. Preheat the air fryer to 360°F (182°C).

4. Place the marinated duck legs in the air fryer basket, skin-side up.

5. Cook for 40 minutes, or until the duck skin is crispy and the meat is tender.

6. Let the duck legs rest for 5 minutes before serving.

**Number of servings:** 2

**Preparation time:** 15 minutes (plus marinating time)

**Cooking time:** 40 minutes

**Nutritional value per serving:** Calories: 480, Carbs: 11g, Fiber: 0g, Sugars: 9g, Protein: 34g, Saturated fat: 12g, Unsaturated fat: 10g

**Difficulty rating:** ★★★☆☆

**Tips for ingredient variations:** For a spicier kick, add a teaspoon of chili flakes to the marinade.

## Organ Meat Pie

**Number of servings:** 6

**Preparation time:** 20 minutes

**Cooking time:** 35 minutes

**Nutritional value per serving:** Calories: 350, Carbs: 15g, Fiber: 1g, Sugars: 2g, Protein: 26g, Saturated fat: 8g, Unsaturated fat: 5g

**Difficulty rating:** ★★★★☆

**Tips for ingredient variations:** For a richer pie, add a layer of mashed potatoes on top of the meat mixture before cooking.

**Directions:**

1. Preheat the air fryer to 350°F (177°C).

2. In a skillet over medium heat, sauté the onion and garlic until translucent. Add the chopped organ meats and cook until browned.

3. Add beef broth, thyme, rosemary, salt, and pepper to the skillet. Simmer until the liquid has reduced by half, about 10 minutes.

4. Place the pre-made pie crust in a compatible air fryer pie dish. Spoon the organ meat mixture into the crust.

5. Place the pie dish in the air fryer basket. Cook for 25 minutes, or until the crust is golden brown and the filling is hot.

6. Let the pie cool for 5 minutes before serving.

**Ingredients:**

- 1 lb mixed organ meats (liver, heart, kidney), finely chopped
- 1 large onion, diced
- 2 cloves garlic, minced
- 1 cup beef broth
- 1 tsp thyme
- 1 tsp rosemary
- Salt and pepper, to taste
- 1 pre-made pie crust

## Bison Prime Rib

**Ingredients:**

- 1 (3 lb) bison prime rib
- 2 tbsp coarse sea salt
- 1 tbsp cracked black pepper
- 2 tsp garlic powder
- 1 tsp onion powder
- 1 tsp dried rosemary

**Directions:**

1. Preheat the air fryer to 390°F (200°C).

2. In a small bowl, mix together the sea salt, cracked black pepper, garlic powder, onion powder, and dried rosemary.

3. Rub the spice mixture all over the bison prime rib, ensuring it is evenly coated.

4. Place the prime rib in the air fryer basket, fat side up.

5. Cook for 60 minutes, or until the prime rib reaches an internal temperature of 135°F (57°C) for medium-rare. Adjust cooking time for desired doneness.

6. Remove the prime rib from the air fryer and let it rest for 10 minutes before slicing.

**Number of servings:** 4

**Preparation time:** 15 minutes

**Cooking time:** 60 minutes

**Nutritional value per serving:** Calories: 690, Carbs: 1g, Fiber: 0g, Sugars: 0g, Protein: 88g, Saturated fat: 20g, Unsaturated fat: 30g

**Difficulty rating:** ★★★☆☆

**Tips for ingredient variations:** For a smoky flavor, add 1 tsp of smoked paprika to the spice mixture.

## Salmon Roast

**Number of servings:** 4

**Preparation time:** 10 minutes

**Cooking time:** 20 minutes

**Nutritional value per serving:** Calories: 345, Carbs: 1g, Fiber: 0g, Sugars: 0g, Protein: 34g, Saturated fat: 5g, Unsaturated fat: 15g

**Difficulty rating:** ★★☆☆☆

**Tips for ingredient variations:** For an Asian twist, substitute olive oil with sesame oil and dill with a teaspoon of grated ginger.

**Directions:**

1. Preheat the air fryer to 360°F (182°C).

2. Rub the salmon fillet with olive oil and then season with minced garlic, sea salt, black pepper, and dried dill.

3. Put the skin-side down seasoned salmon into the air fryer basket. Place slivers of lemon over the fish.

4. Cook for 20 minutes, or until the salmon flakes easily with a fork and reaches an internal temperature of 145°F (63°C).

5. Carefully remove the salmon roast from the air fryer and let it rest for 5 minutes before serving.

**Ingredients:**

- 2 lbs whole salmon fillet
- 2 tbsp olive oil
- 1 lemon, sliced
- 2 garlic cloves, minced
- 1 tsp sea salt
- 1/2 tsp ground black pepper
- 1/2 tsp dried dill

## Whole Trout

**Ingredients:**

- 2 whole trout, cleaned and gutted
- 2 tbsp olive oil
- 1 tsp salt
- 1/2 tsp cracked black pepper
- 1/2 tsp smoked paprika
- 1 lemon, sliced
- Fresh parsley, for garnish

**Directions:**

1. Preheat the air fryer to 400°F (204°C).

2. Rub each trout inside and out with olive oil. Season the inside of each trout with salt, cracked black pepper, and smoked paprika.

3. Place lemon slices inside the cavity of each trout.

4. Place the trout in the air fryer basket, ensuring they are not touching.

5. Cook for 15 minutes, or until the trout skin is crispy and the flesh is flaky.

6. Carefully remove the trout from the air fryer, garnish with fresh parsley, and serve immediately.

**Number of servings:** 2

**Preparation time:** 10 minutes

**Cooking time:** 15 minutes

**Nutritional value per serving:** Calories: 380, Carbs: 1g, Fiber: 0g, Sugars: 0g, Protein: 45g, Saturated fat: 6g, Unsaturated fat: 10g

**Difficulty rating:** ★★★☆☆

**Tips for ingredient variations:** For a citrus herb flavor, add thyme and orange slices to the cavity instead of lemon.

## Shark Bites

**Number of servings:** 4

**Preparation time:** 15 minutes

**Cooking time:** 10 minutes

**Nutritional value per serving:** Calories: 180, Carbs: 1g, Fiber: 0g, Sugars: 0g, Protein: 25g, Saturated fat: 1g, Unsaturated fat: 3g

**Difficulty rating:** ★★★☆☆

**Tips for ingredient variations:** For a spicy twist, add a pinch of cayenne pepper to the seasoning mix.

**Directions:**

1. Preheat the air fryer to 400°F.

2. In a bowl, toss the shark cubes with olive oil, paprika, garlic powder, onion powder, salt, and pepper until evenly coated.

3. Arrange the shark cubes in the air fryer basket in a single layer, ensuring they do not touch.

4. Cook the shark bits for ten minutes, turning them halfway through, or until they are thoroughly cooked and golden brown.

5. Serve immediately with lemon wedges on the side.

**Ingredients:**

- 1 lb shark meat, cut into 1-inch cubes
- 1 tbsp olive oil
- 1 tsp paprika
- 1/2 tsp garlic powder
- 1/2 tsp onion powder
- Salt and pepper, to taste
- Lemon wedges, for serving

# Swordfish Steak

**Ingredients:**

• 2 swordfish steaks (about 6 oz each)

• 2 tbsp olive oil

• 1 tsp dried oregano

• 1 tsp lemon zest

• Salt and pepper, to taste

**Directions:**

1. Preheat the air fryer to 400°F.

2. Brush both sides of the swordfish steaks with olive oil. Season with oregano, lemon zest, salt, and pepper.

3. Place the swordfish steaks in the air fryer basket, ensuring they do not overlap.

4. Cook for 12 minutes, flipping halfway through, until the steaks are cooked through and slightly golden on the outside.

5. Serve immediately, garnished with additional lemon zest if desired.

**Number of servings:** 2

**Preparation time:** 5 minutes

**Cooking time:** 12 minutes

**Nutritional value per serving:** Calories: 280, Carbs: 0g, Fiber: 0g, Sugars: 0g, Protein: 34g, Saturated fat: 4g, Unsaturated fat: 8g

**Difficulty rating:** ★★☆☆☆

**Tips for ingredient variations:** For an Asian flair, marinate the swordfish in a mixture of soy sauce, ginger, and garlic before air frying.

# Tuna Loin

**Number of servings:** 2

**Preparation time:** 10 minutes

**Cooking time:** 8 minutes

**Nutritional value per serving:** Calories: 310, Carbs: 2g, Fiber: 0g, Sugars: 0g, Protein: 45g, Saturated fat: 1g, Unsaturated fat: 5g

**Difficulty rating:** ★★★☆☆

**Tips for ingredient variations:** For a citrusy note, add a tablespoon of orange juice to the soy sauce mixture before brushing it on the tuna.

**Directions:**

1. Preheat the air fryer to 400°F.

2. In a small bowl, mix together soy sauce, sesame oil, and wasabi paste.

3. Brush the mixture over both sides of the tuna loin steaks. Sprinkle with black sesame seeds and salt.

4. Place the tuna steaks in the air fryer basket, ensuring they do not overlap.

5. Cook for 4 minutes, then flip the steaks and cook for an additional 4 minutes for medium-rare, or adjust the cooking time to your preferred doneness.

6. Serve immediately, garnished with additional sesame seeds if desired.

**Ingredients:**

• 2 tuna loin steaks (about 6 oz each)

• 1 tbsp soy sauce

• 1 tbsp sesame oil

• 1/2 tsp wasabi paste

• 1 tsp black sesame seeds

• Salt, to taste

# Chapter 5: Snacks and Side Dishes

These snacks and side dishes showcase the versatility of the carnivore diet, proving that following a meat-centric lifestyle doesn't have to be monotonous. By incorporating a variety of meats and cooking methods, you can enjoy a wide range of flavors and textures that keep your meals exciting and satisfying. Whether you're looking for a quick snack, a hearty side, or a unique dish to share with friends and family, these recipes offer something for every occasion, all while adhering to the principles of the carnivore diet.

## Bacon-Wrapped Asparagus

**Ingredients:**

- 16 asparagus spears, trimmed
- 8 slices of bacon, halved crosswise
- Salt and pepper, to taste

**Directions:**

1. Preheat the air fryer to 400°F (204°C).

2. Season the asparagus spears with salt and pepper.

3. Wrap a half slice of bacon around each spear of asparagus, securing ends if needed.

4. Place the bacon-wrapped asparagus in the air fryer basket in a single layer, ensuring they are not touching.

5. Cook for 12 minutes, or until the bacon is crispy and the asparagus is tender.

6. Serve immediately as a protein-rich side dish or snack.

**Number of servings:** 4

**Preparation time:** 10 minutes

**Cooking time:** 12 minutes

**Nutritional value per serving:** Calories: 120, Carbs: 2g, Fiber: 1g, Sugars: 1g, Protein: 8g, Saturated fat: 3g, Unsaturated fat: 5g

**Difficulty rating:** ★★☆☆☆

**Tips for ingredient variations:** For a smoky flavor, sprinkle some paprika on the bacon before wrapping the asparagus.

## Pork Rind Nachos

**Number of servings:** 4

**Preparation time:** 5 minutes

**Cooking time:** 5 minutes

**Nutritional value per serving:** Calories: 320, Carbs: 2g, Fiber: 0g, Sugars: 1g, Protein: 20g, Saturated fat: 10g, Unsaturated fat: 8g

**Difficulty rating:** ★☆☆☆☆

**Tips for ingredient variations:** Swap out red onions for green onions or add a dollop of guacamole for extra flavor.

**Directions:**

1. Preheat the air fryer to 350°F (177°C).

2. Spread the pork rinds evenly in the air fryer basket.

3. Sprinkle the shredded cheddar cheese and diced jalapeños over the pork rinds.

4. Cook for 5 minutes, or until the cheese is fully melted.

5. After removing the nachos from the air fryer with care, garnish them with chopped red onions and sour cream.

6. Serve immediately as a carnivore-friendly twist on a classic snack.

**Ingredients:**

- 4 cups pork rinds
- 1 cup shredded cheddar cheese
- 1/2 cup diced jalapeños
- 1/2 cup sour cream
- 1/4 cup diced red onions

## Chicken Liver Mousse

**Ingredients:**

- 1 lb chicken livers, cleaned
- 1/4 cup unsalted butter, plus 2 tablespoons for sautéing
- 1 small onion, finely chopped
- 2 cloves garlic, minced
- 1/4 cup heavy cream
- 2 tbsp brandy
- Salt and pepper, to taste
- Thyme leaves for garnish

**Directions:**

1. Preheat the air fryer to 370°F (188°C).

2. In a skillet over medium heat, melt 2 tablespoons of butter. Add the onion and garlic, cooking until soft, about 3 minutes.

3. Add the chicken livers to the skillet and cook for about 5 minutes, or until they are browned on the outside but still have some pink within.

4. Transfer the chicken liver mixture to a food processor, adding the heavy cream, remaining butter, brandy, salt, and pepper. Blend until smooth.

5. Place the mousse in a serving dish and chill in the refrigerator for at least 2 hours before serving.

6. Garnish with thyme leaves and serve with carnivore-friendly crackers or vegetable sticks.

**Number of servings:** 4

**Preparation time:** 15 minutes

**Cooking time:** 10 minutes

**Nutritional value per serving:**
Calories: 310, Carbs: 3g, Fiber: 0g, Sugars: 1g, Protein: 20g, Saturated fat: 15g, Unsaturated fat: 7g

**Difficulty rating:** ★★★☆☆

**Tips for ingredient variations:**
For a different flavor profile, substitute brandy with cognac or add a pinch of nutmeg.

## Beef Jerky

**Number of servings:** 4

**Preparation time:** 8 hours (includes marinating time)

**Cooking time:** 4 hours

**Nutritional value per serving:**
Calories: 310, Carbs: 9g, Fiber: 0g, Sugars: 6g, Protein: 44g, Saturated fat: 3g, Unsaturated fat: 2g

**Difficulty rating:** ★★★☆☆

**Tips for ingredient variations:**
For a sweeter jerky, increase the brown sugar to 1/4 cup. For a teriyaki twist, add 1 tbsp of sesame oil and replace brown sugar with honey.

**Directions:**

1. Mix together soy sauce, Worcestershire sauce, brown sugar, smoked paprika, onion and garlic powders, black pepper, and red pepper flakes in a mixing bowl. Until the sugar is completely dissolved, stir.

2. Make sure that every piece of thinly sliced beef is well-coated by adding it to the marinade. For optimal flavor, cover and refrigerate for at least eight hours, or overnight.

3. Preheat the air fryer to 180°F.

4. Remove the beef slices from the marinade and pat dry with paper towels. Arrange the beef slices in a single layer in the air fryer basket, ensuring they do not overlap.

5. Cook until the jerky is chewy and dry, about 4 hours.

6. Let the jerky cool before storing in an airtight container.

**Ingredients:**

- 2 lbs beef flank steak, thinly sliced
- 1/2 cup soy sauce
- 1/4 cup Worcestershire sauce
- 2 tbsp brown sugar
- 2 tsp smoked paprika
- 1 tsp garlic powder
- 1 tsp onion powder
- 1/2 tsp black pepper
- 1/4 tsp red pepper flakes (optional for extra heat)

## Lamb Meatballs

**Ingredients:**

- 1 lb ground lamb
- 1/4 cup almond flour
- 1 large egg
- 2 cloves garlic, minced
- 1 tsp cumin
- 1 tsp smoked paprika
- 1/2 tsp salt
- 1/4 tsp black pepper
- 1/4 cup fresh parsley, finely chopped

**Directions:**

1. In a large bowl, combine ground lamb, almond flour, egg, minced garlic, cumin, smoked paprika, salt, black pepper, and parsley. Mix until well combined.

2. Create 1-inch meatballs out of the mixture.

3. Preheat the air fryer to 400°F.

4. Arrange the meatballs in the air fryer basket, ensuring they are not touching.

5. Cook for 15 minutes, or until the meatballs are browned on the outside and cooked through.

6. Serve hot, garnished with additional fresh parsley if desired.

**Number of servings:** 4

**Preparation time:** 15 minutes

**Cooking time:** 15 minutes

**Nutritional value per serving:** Calories: 330, Carbs: 3g, Fiber: 1g, Sugars: 0g, Protein: 20g, Saturated fat: 15g, Unsaturated fat: 10g

**Difficulty rating:** ★★☆☆☆

**Tips for ingredient variations:** For a Mediterranean flair, add 1/4 cup of crumbled feta cheese to the meatball mixture. For a spicy version, include 1/2 tsp of chili flakes.

## Turkey Jerky

**Ingredients:**

- 2 lbs turkey breast, thinly sliced
- 1/2 cup low-sodium soy sauce
- 1/4 cup apple cider vinegar
- 2 tbsp honey
- 1 tsp ground ginger
- 1 tsp garlic powder
- 1/2 tsp ground black pepper
- 1/4 tsp liquid smoke (optional)

**Directions:**

1. In a mixing bowl, whisk together low-sodium soy sauce, apple cider vinegar, honey, ground ginger, garlic powder, ground black pepper, and liquid smoke until well combined.

2. Make sure every slice of turkey is thoroughly coated by adding it to the marinade in thin slices. For at least eight hours, or overnight, cover and chill.

3. Preheat the air fryer to 180°F.

4. After removing the turkey slices from the marinade, use paper towels to pat dry. Make sure the turkey slices do not overlap when you arrange them in the air fryer basket in a single layer.

5. Cook for 4 hours, or until the jerky is dry and chewy.

6. Let the jerky cool before storing in an airtight container.

**Number of servings:** 4

**Preparation time:** 8 hours (includes marinating time)

**Cooking time:** 4 hours

**Nutritional value per serving:** Calories: 280, Carbs: 10g, Fiber: 0g, Sugars: 8g, Protein: 40g, Saturated fat: 1g, Unsaturated fat: 1g

**Difficulty rating:** ★★★☆☆

**Tips for ingredient variations:** For a spicier jerky, add 1 tsp of crushed red pepper flakes to the marinade. For a sweeter version, increase the honey to 1/4 cup.

## Bison Bites

**Ingredients:**

- 1 lb bison flank steak, cut into 1-inch cubes
- 1 tbsp olive oil
- 1 tsp sea salt
- 1/2 tsp ground black pepper
- 1/2 tsp garlic powder
- 1/2 tsp onion powder

**Directions:**

1. Preheat the air fryer to 400°F.

2. The bison cubes should be equally coated after being tossed in a bowl containing olive oil, sea salt, ground black pepper, garlic powder, and onion powder.

3. Arrange the bison cubes in the air fryer basket in a single layer, ensuring they do not touch.

4. Cook for 15 minutes, shaking the basket halfway through the cooking time, until the bison bites are browned and cooked to your desired doneness.

5. Serve immediately.

**Number of servings:** 4

**Preparation time:** 10 minutes

**Cooking time:** 15 minutes

**Nutritional value per serving:** Calories: 220, Carbs: 0g, Fiber: 0g, Sugars: 0g, Protein: 25g, Saturated fat: 3g, Unsaturated fat: 2g

**Difficulty rating:** ★★☆☆☆

**Tips for ingredient variations:** For a spicy kick, add 1/4 tsp of cayenne pepper to the seasoning mix.

---

## Venison Jerky

**Ingredients:**

- 1 lb venison, thinly sliced
- 1/2 cup soy sauce
- 1/4 cup Worcestershire sauce
- 2 tbsp brown sugar
- 1 tsp black pepper
- 1 tsp smoked paprika
- 1/2 tsp garlic powder
- 1/2 tsp onion powder

**Directions:**

1. In a bowl, whisk together soy sauce, Worcestershire sauce, brown sugar, black pepper, smoked paprika, garlic powder, and onion powder.

2. Make sure every piece of thinly sliced venison is well coated by adding it to the marinade. For at least eight hours, or overnight, cover and chill.

3. Preheat the air fryer to 160°F.

4. Remove the venison slices from the marinade and place them in the air fryer basket in a single layer, ensuring they do not overlap.

5. Cook for 4 hours, or until the jerky is dry and chewy.

6. Let the jerky cool before storing in an airtight container.

**Number of servings:** 4

**Preparation time:** 8 hours (includes marinating time)

**Cooking time:** 4 hours

**Nutritional value per serving:** Calories: 180, Carbs: 9g, Fiber: 0g, Sugars: 6g, Protein: 24g, Saturated fat: 1g, Unsaturated fat: 0.5g

**Difficulty rating:** ★★★★☆

**Tips for ingredient variations:** For a sweeter jerky, increase the amount of brown sugar to 1/3 cup. For a spicier jerky, add 1 tsp of red chili flakes to the marinade.

## Elk Sausage

**Ingredients:**

- 1 lb ground elk meat
- 1 tsp sage
- 1/2 tsp thyme
- 1/4 tsp nutmeg
- 1/4 tsp cayenne pepper
- 1 tsp sea salt
- 1/2 tsp ground black pepper
- 2 tbsp olive oil (for cooking)

**Directions:**

1. In a large bowl, combine ground elk meat, sage, thyme, nutmeg, cayenne pepper, sea salt, and black pepper. Ensure that all the components are well combined and dispersed.

2. Form the mixture into 8 sausages, about 4 inches long and 1 inch thick.

3. Preheat the air fryer to 370°F.

4. Brush each sausage lightly with olive oil and place them in the air fryer basket, ensuring they are not touching.

5. Cook for 15 minutes, turning the sausages halfway through the cooking time, until they are browned and cooked through.

6. Serve immediately.

**Number of servings:** 4

**Preparation time:** 20 minutes

**Cooking time:** 15 minutes

**Nutritional value per serving:** Calories: 240, Carbs: 0g, Fiber: 0g, Sugars: 0g, Protein: 26g, Saturated fat: 5g, Unsaturated fat: 3g

**Difficulty rating:** ★★★☆☆

**Tips for ingredient variations:** For a more aromatic sausage, add 1 tsp of finely chopped garlic or 1/4 cup of finely diced onion to the meat mixture.

## Rabbit Jerky

**Number of servings:** 4

**Preparation time:** 8 hours (includes marinating time)

**Cooking time:** 4 hours

**Nutritional value per serving:** Calories: 180, Carbs: 3g, Fiber: 0g, Sugars: 1g, Protein: 25g, Saturated fat: 0.5g, Unsaturated fat: 1g

**Difficulty rating:** ★★★★☆

**Tips for ingredient variations:** For a sweeter jerky, add 1 tbsp of honey or maple syrup to the marinade.

**Directions:**

1. In a bowl, combine soy sauce, Worcestershire sauce, apple cider vinegar, smoked paprika, garlic powder, onion powder, black pepper, and cayenne pepper (if using) to create the marinade.

2. Add the thinly sliced rabbit meat to the marinade, ensuring each piece is well-coated. Cover and refrigerate for at least 8 hours, or overnight.

3. Preheat the air fryer to 180°F.

4. Remove the rabbit slices from the marinade and place them in the air fryer basket in a single layer, ensuring they do not overlap.

5. Cook for 4 hours, or until the jerky is dry and chewy.

6. Let the jerky cool before storing in an airtight container.

**Ingredients:**

- 1 lb rabbit meat, thinly sliced
- 1/2 cup soy sauce
- 1/4 cup Worcestershire sauce
- 2 tbsp apple cider vinegar
- 1 tbsp smoked paprika
- 1 tsp garlic powder
- 1 tsp onion powder
- 1/2 tsp black pepper
- 1/4 tsp cayenne pepper (optional)

## Goose Liver Pâté

**Ingredients:**

- 1 lb goose liver, cleaned and trimmed
- 1/4 cup unsalted butter
- 1 small onion, finely chopped
- 2 cloves garlic, minced
- 1/4 cup brandy
- 1/2 cup heavy cream
- 1 tsp thyme, dried
- Salt and pepper, to taste

**Directions:**

1. In a skillet over medium heat, melt half of the butter. Add the onion and garlic, cooking until soft and translucent, about 3 minutes.

2. Add the goose liver to the skillet, cooking until browned on all sides.

3. Pour in the brandy and allow to simmer for 2 minutes.

4. Transfer the liver mixture to a food processor, adding the heavy cream, remaining butter, thyme, salt, and pepper. Blend until smooth.

5. Spoon the pâté into a serving dish or individual ramekins. Cover and refrigerate for at least 2 hours, or until set.

6. Serve chilled with carnivore-friendly bread or vegetable sticks.

**Number of servings:** 6

**Preparation time:** 15 minutes

**Cooking time:** 2 hours

**Nutritional value per serving:** Calories: 310, Carbs: 2g, Fiber: 0g, Sugars: 1g, Protein: 14g, Saturated fat: 18g, Unsaturated fat: 7g

**Difficulty rating:** ★★★☆☆

**Tips for ingredient variations:** For a richer flavor, substitute brandy with cognac or add a pinch of nutmeg.

## Quail Legs

**Number of servings:** 4

**Preparation time:** 10 minutes

**Cooking time:** 15 minutes

**Nutritional value per serving:** Calories: 210, Carbs: 1g, Fiber: 0g, Sugars: 0g, Protein: 24g, Saturated fat: 3g, Unsaturated fat: 5g

**Difficulty rating:** ★★☆☆☆

**Tips for ingredient variations:** For a spicy twist, add a pinch of cayenne pepper to the seasoning mix before coating the quail legs.

**Directions:**

1. Preheat the air fryer to 400°F.

2. In a bowl, toss the quail legs with olive oil, smoked paprika, garlic powder, salt, and pepper until evenly coated.

3. Arrange the quail legs in the air fryer basket in a single layer, ensuring they do not touch.

4. Cook for 15 minutes, or until the quail legs are golden brown and crispy.

5. Before serving, garnish with freshly cut parsley.

**Ingredients:**

- 16 quail legs
- 2 tbsp olive oil
- 1 tsp smoked paprika
- 1 tsp garlic powder
- Salt and pepper, to taste
- Fresh parsley, chopped (for garnish)

## Lamb Bacon

**Ingredients:**

• 1 lb lamb belly, sliced into 1/4-inch thick strips

• 1 tsp sea salt

• 1/2 tsp black pepper

• 1 tsp rosemary, finely chopped

• 1/2 tsp garlic powder

**Directions:**

1. Preheat the air fryer to 400°F (204°C).

2. In a small bowl, mix together sea salt, black pepper, rosemary, and garlic powder.

3. Rub the spice mixture evenly onto both sides of each lamb belly strip.

4. Place the seasoned lamb strips in the air fryer basket, ensuring they do not overlap.

5. Cook for 15 minutes, or until the lamb bacon is crispy, flipping halfway through the cooking time.

6. Remove the lamb bacon from the air fryer and let it cool on a paper towel-lined plate to drain any excess fat.

**Number of servings:** 4

**Preparation time:** 10 minutes

**Cooking time:** 15 minutes

**Nutritional value per serving:** Calories: 290, Carbs: 0g, Fiber: 0g, Sugars: 0g, Protein: 19g, Saturated fat: 22g, Unsaturated fat: 8g

**Difficulty rating:** ★★☆☆☆

**Tips for ingredient variations:** For a sweeter version, sprinkle a little bit of brown sugar on the lamb strips before cooking.

## Beef Tallow Fries

**Number of servings:** 4

**Preparation time:** 10 minutes

**Cooking time:** 20 minutes

**Nutritional value per serving:** Calories: 310, Carbs: 45g, Fiber: 3g, Sugars: 2g, Protein: 4g, Saturated fat: 7g, Unsaturated fat: 5g

**Difficulty rating:** ★★☆☆☆

**Tips for ingredient variations:** For added flavor, sprinkle some garlic powder or paprika on the fries before cooking.

**Directions:**

1. Preheat the air fryer to 380°F (193°C).

2. In a large bowl, toss the potato sticks with melted beef tallow, ensuring each stick is well coated.

3. Season the potatoes with sea salt and cracked black pepper, tossing again to distribute the seasoning evenly.

4. Place the potato sticks in the air fryer basket in a single layer, working in batches if necessary.

5. Cook until the fries are crispy and golden brown, shaking the basket halfway through the 20 minutes.

6. Present right away.

**Ingredients:**

• 2 lbs russet potatoes, peeled and cut into 1/4-inch sticks

• 1/4 cup beef tallow, melted

• 1 tsp sea salt

• 1/2 tsp cracked black pepper

## Pork Cracklings

**Ingredients:**

- 1 lb pork skin, cut into 1-inch squares
- 1 tsp salt
- 1/2 tsp smoked paprika

**Directions:**

1. Preheat the air fryer to 400°F (204°C).

2. In a bowl, season the pork skin squares with salt and smoked paprika, tossing to ensure each piece is evenly coated.

3. Place the pork skin squares in the air fryer basket in a single layer, ensuring they do not overlap.

4. Cook for 15 minutes, or until the cracklings are puffed up and crispy.

5. Remove the pork cracklings from the air fryer and let them cool on a paper towel-lined plate to drain any excess fat.

6. Serve immediately as a crunchy snack.

**Number of servings:** 4

**Preparation time:** 5 minutes

**Cooking time:** 15 minutes

**Nutritional value per serving:** Calories: 240, Carbs: 0g, Fiber: 0g, Sugars: 0g, Protein: 22g, Saturated fat: 14g, Unsaturated fat: 10g

**Difficulty rating:** ★☆☆☆

**Tips for ingredient variations:** For a spicy kick, add a pinch of cayenne pepper to the seasoning mix before cooking.

## Chicken Skins

**Number of servings:** 4

**Preparation time:** 5 minutes

**Cooking time:** 15 minutes

**Nutritional value per serving:** Calories: 100, Carbs: 0g, Fiber: 0g, Sugars: 0g, Protein: 9g, Saturated fat: 3g, Unsaturated fat: 2g

**Difficulty rating:** ★★☆☆

**Tips for ingredient variations:** For a spicy version, add 1/4 tsp of cayenne pepper to the seasoning mix.

**Directions:**

1. Preheat the air fryer to 400°F (204°C).

2. In a bowl, mix the chicken skins with salt, black pepper, and smoked paprika until evenly coated.

3. Arrange the chicken skins in a single layer in the air fryer basket, ensuring they do not overlap.

4. Cook for 15 minutes, or until the skins are crispy and golden brown.

5. Remove from the air fryer and let them cool on a paper towel to drain any excess fat.

**Ingredients:**

- Chicken skins from 4 chicken thighs
- 1 tsp salt
- 1/2 tsp black pepper
- 1/2 tsp smoked paprika

## Duck Fat Chips

**Ingredients:**

• 2 large russet potatoes, peeled and sliced into thin chips

• 2 tbsp duck fat, melted

• 1 tsp sea salt

• 1/2 tsp ground black pepper

**Directions:**

1. Preheat the air fryer to 380°F (193°C).

2. In a large bowl, toss the potato slices with melted duck fat, sea salt, and black pepper until well coated.

3. Arrange the potato slices in a single layer in the air fryer basket, working in batches if necessary.

4. Cook for 20 minutes, flipping the chips halfway through, until they are crispy and golden brown.

5. Remove from the air fryer and let them cool on a paper towel to drain any excess fat.

**Number of servings:** 4

**Preparation time:** 10 minutes

**Cooking time:** 20 minutes

**Nutritional value per serving:** Calories: 210, Carbs: 37g, Fiber: 2g, Sugars: 1g, Protein: 4g, Saturated fat: 3g, Unsaturated fat: 1g

**Difficulty rating:** ★★★☆☆

**Tips for ingredient variations:** For added flavor, sprinkle freshly chopped rosemary or thyme over the chips before serving.

## Liver Chips

**Number of servings:** 4

**Preparation time:** 15 minutes

**Cooking time:** 10 minutes

**Nutritional value per serving:** Calories: 180, Carbs: 1g, Fiber: 0g, Sugars: 0g, Protein: 27g, Saturated fat: 2g, Unsaturated fat: 3g

**Difficulty rating:** ★★★★☆

**Tips for ingredient variations:** For a smoky flavor, add 1/2 tsp of smoked paprika to the seasoning mix.

**Directions:**

1. Preheat the air fryer to 400°F (204°C).

2. In a bowl, toss the thinly sliced beef liver with olive oil, salt, garlic powder, and cayenne pepper until well coated.

3. Arrange the liver slices in a single layer in the air fryer basket, working in batches if necessary.

4. Cook for 10 minutes, or until the liver chips are crispy.

5. Remove from the air fryer and let them cool on a paper towel to drain any excess oil.

**Ingredients:**

• 1 lb beef liver, thinly sliced

• 2 tbsp olive oil

• 1 tsp salt

• 1/2 tsp garlic powder

• 1/4 tsp cayenne pepper

## Bison Bone Broth

**Ingredients:**

• 4 lbs bison bones, preferably a mix of marrow bones and bones with a bit of meat

• 2 carrots, chopped

• 2 celery stalks, chopped

• 1 large onion, quartered

• 4 cloves of garlic, smashed

• 2 bay leaves

• 1 tablespoon apple cider vinegar

• 1 teaspoon salt

• 1/2 teaspoon black pepper

• Water, enough to cover the bones

**Directions:**

1. Preheat your air fryer to 400°F (if it has a roast setting) and roast the bison bones for 30 minutes until they are well-browned. This step may need to be done in batches depending on the size of your air fryer.

2. Transfer the roasted bones to a large slow cooker. Add the carrots, celery, onion, garlic, bay leaves, apple cider vinegar, salt, and pepper.

3. Add enough water to cover the bones completely.

4. Set the slow cooker to low and cook for 24 hours, adding water as necessary to keep the bones submerged.

5. After 24 hours, strain the broth through a fine-mesh sieve into a large container, discarding the solids.

6. Allow the broth to cool, then refrigerate. Once chilled, remove the solidified fat from the top.

7. Reheat the broth as needed and serve.

**Number of servings:** 8

**Preparation time:** 10 minutes

**Cooking time:** 24 hours

**Nutritional value per serving:** Calories: 50, Carbs: 2g, Fiber: 0.5g, Sugars: 1g, Protein: 7g, Saturated fat: 0g, Unsaturated fat: 0g

**Difficulty rating:** ★★☆☆☆

**Tips for ingredient variations:** For a deeper flavor, add a piece of kombu or a few dried mushrooms to the pot before cooking.

## Salmon Skin Chips

**Number of servings:** 4

**Preparation time:** 5 minutes

**Cooking time:** 10 minutes

**Nutritional value per serving:** Calories: 58, Carbs: 0g, Fiber: 0g, Sugars: 0g, Protein: 6g, Saturated fat: 1g, Unsaturated fat: 2g

**Difficulty rating:** ★☆☆☆☆

**Tips for ingredient variations:** Experiment with different seasonings like lemon zest and dill for a fresh twist or chili powder for a spicy kick.

**Directions:**

1. Preheat your air fryer to 360°F (182°C).

2. Remove any remaining flesh from the salmon skins and cut them into bite-sized pieces.

3. Toss the salmon skin pieces with olive oil and salt, ensuring they are evenly coated. Add any additional seasonings as desired.

4. Place the salmon skin pieces in the air fryer basket in a single layer, ensuring they do not overlap.

5. Cook for 10 minutes, or until crispy and golden brown. To ensure uniform crispy frying, shake the basket halfway through.

6. Remove the salmon skin chips from the air fryer and let them cool on a paper towel to absorb any excess oil.

7. Serve immediately as a crunchy snack or garnish.

**Ingredients:**

• Skin from 4 salmon fillets

• 1 tablespoon olive oil

• Salt, to taste

• Optional seasonings: paprika, garlic powder, or black pepper

## Trout Jerky

**Ingredients:**

• 1 lb trout fillets, skin removed

• 1/4 cup soy sauce

• 2 tablespoons maple syrup

• 1 tablespoon apple cider vinegar

• 1 teaspoon smoked paprika

• 1/2 teaspoon garlic powder

• 1/2 teaspoon onion powder

• 1/4 teaspoon black pepper

**Directions:**

1. Slice the trout fillets into thin strips, approximately 1/4 inch thick.

2. In a bowl, whisk together soy sauce, maple syrup, apple cider vinegar, smoked paprika, garlic powder, onion powder, and black pepper to create the marinade.

3. Add the trout strips to the marinade, ensuring each piece is well-coated. Cover and refrigerate for at least 4 hours, or overnight for best results.

4. Preheat your air fryer to 160°F (71°C), or the lowest setting available.

5. Remove the trout strips from the marinade and gently pat them dry with paper towels.

6. Arrange the trout strips in the air fryer basket in a single layer, ensuring they do not touch.

7. Cook for 4 hours, or until the trout jerky is dry and chewy. Check periodically and remove any pieces that dry faster.

8. Let the trout jerky cool before storing in an airtight container.

**Number of servings:** 4

**Preparation time:** 30 minutes (plus 4 hours marinating time)

**Cooking time:** 4 hours

**Nutritional value per serving:** Calories: 120, Carbs: 6g, Fiber: 0g, Sugars: 5g, Protein: 17g, Saturated fat: 0g, Unsaturated fat: 1g

**Difficulty rating:** ★★★☆☆

**Tips for ingredient variations:** For a spicier jerky, add a teaspoon of chili flakes or a splash of hot sauce to the marinade.

---

## Shark Fin Soup

**Number of servings:** 4

**Preparation time:** 15 minutes

**Cooking time:** 2 hours

**Nutritional value per serving:** Calories: 180, Carbs: 5g, Fiber: 0g, Sugars: 1g, Protein: 25g, Saturated fat: 1g, Unsaturated fat: 2g

**Difficulty rating:** ★★★★☆

**Tips for ingredient variations:** For a more complex flavor, add a splash of Shaoxing wine during step 1.

**Directions:**

1. In a large pot, bring the chicken broth to a boil. Add the soy sauce, oyster sauce, sesame oil, ginger slices, and scallions.

2. Reduce the heat to low and add the shark fins. Simmer for 1.5 hours, ensuring the fins become tender.

3. Gradually stir in the cornstarch slurry, stirring constantly until the soup thickens slightly.

4. Season with salt and white pepper to taste.

5. Serve hot, garnished with additional chopped scallions if desired.

**Ingredients:**

• 1 lb shark fins (pre-cleaned and prepared)

• 8 cups chicken broth

• 1 tablespoon soy sauce

• 1 tablespoon oyster sauce

• 2 teaspoons sesame oil

• 1 small piece of ginger, thinly sliced

• 2 scallions, chopped

• Salt and white pepper, to taste

• Cornstarch slurry (2 tablespoons cornstarch mixed with 4 tablespoons water)

## Swordfish Bites

**Ingredients:**

• 1 lb swordfish steak, cut into 1-inch cubes

• 2 tablespoons olive oil

• 1 teaspoon lemon zest

• 1 teaspoon dried thyme

• 1/2 teaspoon garlic powder

• Salt and pepper, to taste

• Lemon wedges, for serving

**Directions:**

1. Preheat the air fryer to 400°F.

2. In a bowl, combine olive oil, lemon zest, dried thyme, garlic powder, salt, and pepper. Add the swordfish cubes and toss to coat evenly.

3. Arrange the swordfish cubes in the air fryer basket in a single layer, ensuring they do not touch.

4. Cook for 8 minutes, flipping halfway through, until the swordfish is cooked through and slightly golden on the outside.

5. Serve immediately with lemon wedges on the side.

**Number of servings:** 4

**Preparation time:** 10 minutes

**Cooking time:** 8 minutes

**Nutritional value per serving:** Calories: 220, Carbs: 1g, Fiber: 0g, Sugars: 0g, Protein: 23g, Saturated fat: 3g, Unsaturated fat: 5g

**Difficulty rating:** ★★★☆☆

**Tips for ingredient variations:** For a spicy twist, add a pinch of cayenne pepper to the olive oil mixture before coating the swordfish.

## Tuna Salad

**Number of servings:** 4

**Preparation time:** 10 minutes

**Cooking time:** 0 minutes

**Nutritional value per serving:** Calories: 180, Carbs: 2g, Fiber: 0.5g, Sugars: 1g, Protein: 20g, Saturated fat: 2g, Unsaturated fat: 5g

**Difficulty rating:** ★☆☆☆☆

**Tips for ingredient variations:** For added crunch, include diced cucumber or apple in the tuna salad.

**Directions:**

1. In a large bowl, mix together the drained tuna, mayonnaise, chopped celery, red onion, capers, lemon juice, and Dijon mustard until well combined.

2. Season with salt and pepper to taste.

3. Chill the tuna salad in the refrigerator for at least 30 minutes before serving.

4. Serve the tuna salad on lettuce leaves.

**Ingredients:**

• 2 cans (6 oz each) tuna in olive oil, drained

• 1/4 cup mayonnaise

• 1 celery stalk, finely chopped

• 2 tablespoons red onion, finely chopped

• 1 tablespoon capers, drained

• 1 tablespoon lemon juice

• Salt and pepper, to taste

• 1 teaspoon Dijon mustard

• 4 lettuce leaves, for serving

# Chapter 6: Special Occasion Feasts

Special occasions call for extraordinary meals that bring together family and friends to celebrate milestones, holidays, or simply the joy of shared company. While the carnivore diet emphasizes simplicity and the nutritional powerhouse of meat, it also offers a canvas for culinary creativity, especially when it comes to feasting. With your air fryer by your side, preparing a special occasion feast that remains true to the carnivore ethos is not only possible but promises to be an unforgettable experience.

These special occasion feasts demonstrate the versatility and culinary potential of the carnivore diet, proving that celebrating with a meat-centric menu can be both luxurious and satisfying. With the air fryer, preparing these dishes is not only efficient but also ensures each meal is cooked to perfection, allowing you to enjoy the celebration without spending all day in the kitchen. Whether you're hosting a holiday dinner, a birthday party, or an intimate gathering, these recipes offer something special for every occasion, making every meal a memorable feast.

## Beef Wellington

**Ingredients:**

- 2 lbs beef tenderloin
- 2 tbsp olive oil
- Salt and pepper, to taste
- 4 tbsp Dijon mustard
- 8 slices prosciutto
- 1/2 lb mushroom duxelles (finely chopped mushrooms sautéed with onions and garlic)
- 1 puff pastry sheet, thawed
- 1 egg, beaten for egg wash

**Directions:**

1. Preheat the air fryer to 400°F (204°C).

2. Add salt and pepper to the beef tenderloin to season it. Sear the beef in olive oil in a skillet over high heat, making sure to brown it on both sides. After letting cool, coat everything with Dijon mustard.

3. Arrange the slices of prosciutto, slightly overlapping, on a sheet of plastic wrap. After the prosciutto has cooled, lay the cold beef tenderloin on top of the mushroom duxelles. Tightly roll the prosciutto and duxelles around the steak using the plastic wrap. Put in the fridge for fifteen minutes.

4. Roll out the puff pastry on a floured surface. Place the steak in the middle of the pastry after removing it from the plastic wrap. Trim any excess pastry before folding it over the steak and sealing the edges. Use the beaten egg to coat the entire pastry.

5. When the pastry is golden brown, or after 25 minutes for medium-rare, place the Beef Wellington in the air fryer basket.

6. Let rest for 10 minutes before slicing and serving.

**Number of servings:** 4

**Preparation time:** 30 minutes

**Cooking time:** 45 minutes

**Nutritional value per serving:** Calories: 760, Carbs: 24g, Fiber: 2g, Sugars: 2g, Protein: 52g, Saturated fat: 14g, Unsaturated fat: 22g

**Difficulty rating:** ★★★★☆

**Tips for ingredient variations:** For an added layer of flavor, include a layer of blanched spinach between the prosciutto and mushroom duxelles.

## Rack of Lamb

**Number of servings:** 4

**Preparation time:** 20 minutes

**Cooking time:** 20 minutes

**Nutritional value per serving:** Calories: 495, Carbs: 15g, Fiber: 1g, Sugars: 2g, Protein: 38g, Saturated fat: 9g, Unsaturated fat: 12g

**Difficulty rating:** ★★★☆☆

**Tips for ingredient variations:** For a gluten-free version, substitute breadcrumbs with crushed almonds or pistachios for a crunchy crust.

**Directions:**

1. Preheat the air fryer to 400°F (204°C).

2. Season the rack of lamb with salt and pepper. In a skillet over medium heat, brown the lamb on all sides in olive oil. Let cool slightly.

3. In a small bowl, mix together the rosemary, thyme, and garlic. Rub this herb mixture all over the lamb.

4. Brush the lamb with Dijon mustard, then press the breadcrumbs onto the mustard-coated lamb to adhere.

5. Place the rack of lamb in the air fryer basket, fat side up. Cook for 15-20 minutes, or until the breadcrumbs are golden and the lamb reaches your desired doneness (145°F for medium-rare).

6. Let the lamb rest for 5 minutes before cutting into individual ribs and serving.

**Ingredients:**

- 1 rack of lamb (about 8 ribs)
- 2 tbsp olive oil
- Salt and pepper, to taste
- 2 tsp rosemary, minced
- 2 tsp thyme, minced
- 4 cloves garlic, minced
- 1/4 cup Dijon mustard
- 1 cup breadcrumbs

## Pork Crown Roast

**Ingredients:**

• 1 pork crown roast (about 12 ribs)

• 2 tbsp olive oil

• Salt and pepper, to taste

• 2 tsp sage, minced

• 2 tsp rosemary, minced

• 4 cloves garlic, minced

• 1/2 cup dry white wine

• 2 apples, cored and sliced

• 1 onion, sliced

**Directions:**

1. Preheat the air fryer to 325°F (163°C).

2. Rub the pork crown roast all over with olive oil, then season with salt, pepper, sage, rosemary, and garlic.

3. Place the crown roast in the air fryer basket. Pour the white wine into the bottom of the basket. Scatter the apple and onion slices around the roast.

4. Cook for 2 hours, or until the internal temperature of the pork reaches 145°F (63°C).

5. Remove the pork crown roast from the air fryer and let it rest for 10 minutes before slicing. Serve with the roasted apples and onions.

**Number of servings:** 8

**Preparation time:** 30 minutes

**Cooking time:** 2 hours

**Nutritional value per serving:** Calories: 310, Carbs: 8g, Fiber: 1g, Sugars: 5g, Protein: 45g, Saturated fat: 5g, Unsaturated fat: 8g

**Difficulty rating:** ★★★★☆

**Tips for ingredient variations:** For added sweetness, sprinkle brown sugar over the apples and onions before cooking.

## Whole Duck

**Number of servings:** 4

**Preparation time:** 20 minutes

**Cooking time:** 60 minutes

**Nutritional value per serving:** Calories: 620, Carbs: 5g, Fiber: 1g, Sugars: 3g, Protein: 45g, Saturated fat: 17g, Unsaturated fat: 20g

**Difficulty rating:** ★★★☆☆

**Tips for ingredient variations:** For a different citrus note, substitute orange with lemon or lime.

**Directions:**

1. Preheat the air fryer to 350°F (177°C).

2. Rinse the duck inside and out, then pat dry with paper towels.

3. Season the duck inside and out with sea salt and black pepper.

4. Stuff the cavity of the duck with the orange quarters and fresh thyme sprigs.

5. Rub the outside of the duck with olive oil.

6. Place the duck breast side down in the air fryer basket. Cook for 30 minutes.

7. Flip the duck so it's breast side up and cook for an additional 30 minutes, or until the skin is crispy and a meat thermometer inserted into the thickest part of the thigh reads 165°F (74°C).

8. Let the duck rest for 10 minutes before carving.

**Ingredients:**

• 1 whole duck (about 5 lbs)

• 2 tbsp sea salt

• 1 tbsp black pepper

• 1 orange, quartered

• 4 sprigs of fresh thyme

• 2 tbsp olive oil

## Roasted Turkey

**Ingredients:**

• 1 whole turkey (about 10 lbs), thawed

• 4 tbsp unsalted butter, softened

• 2 tsp salt

• 1 tsp ground black pepper

• 1 tbsp dried rosemary

• 1 tbsp dried thyme

• 1 large onion, quartered

• 4 cloves garlic, smashed

**Directions:**

1. Preheat the air fryer to 325°F (163°C).

2. Remove the giblets and neck from the turkey, rinse the turkey inside and out, and pat dry with paper towels.

3. Mix the softened butter with salt, black pepper, rosemary, and thyme. Rub this mixture under the skin and all over the outside of the turkey.

4. Place the onion quarters and smashed garlic cloves inside the turkey cavity.

5. Use kitchen twine to truss the legs together, then tuck the tips of the wings under the body.

6. In the air fryer basket, place the turkey breast side up. After 90 minutes of cooking, the flesh should register 165°F (74°C) on a meat thermometer put into the thickest section of the thigh. The turkey can brown too soon, in which case you might need to cover it with aluminum foil.

7. Let the turkey rest for 20 minutes before carving.

**Number of servings:** 8

**Preparation time:** 30 minutes

**Cooking time:** 90 minutes

**Nutritional value per serving:** Calories: 690, Carbs: 3g, Fiber: 1g, Sugars: 1g, Protein: 95g, Saturated fat: 8g, Unsaturated fat: 10g

**Difficulty rating:** ★★★★☆

**Tips for ingredient variations:** For added flavor, insert slices of lemon or apple inside the turkey cavity along with the onion and garlic.

## Bison Tomahawk Steak

**Number of servings:** 2

**Preparation time:** 5 minutes

**Cooking time:** 15 minutes

**Nutritional value per serving:** Calories: 560, Carbs: 1g, Fiber: 0g, Sugars: 0g, Protein: 82g, Saturated fat: 9g, Unsaturated fat: 15g

**Difficulty rating:** ★★★☆☆

**Tips for ingredient variations:** For a smoky flavor, add 1/2 tsp of smoked paprika to the seasoning mix.

**Directions:**

1. Preheat the air fryer to 400°F (204°C).

2. Rub each steak with olive oil, then season both sides with sea salt, cracked black pepper, garlic powder, and onion powder.

3. Place the steaks in the air fryer basket, ensuring they do not overlap.

4. Cook for 7 minutes, then flip the steaks and cook for an additional 8 minutes for medium-rare, or adjust the cooking time to your preferred doneness.

5. Let the steaks rest for 5 minutes before serving.

**Ingredients:**

• 2 bison tomahawk steaks (about 1 lb each)

• 2 tbsp olive oil

• 2 tsp coarse sea salt

• 1 tsp cracked black pepper

• 1 tsp garlic powder

• 1 tsp onion powder

# Venison Tenderloin

**Ingredients:**

• 2 venison tenderloins (about 6 oz each)

• 1 tbsp olive oil

• 1 tsp sea salt

• 1/2 tsp cracked black pepper

• 1 tsp dried rosemary

• 1/2 tsp garlic powder

**Directions:**

1. Preheat the air fryer to 400°F.

2. Rub each venison tenderloin with olive oil, then season with sea salt, cracked black pepper, dried rosemary, and garlic powder.

3. Place the tenderloins in the air fryer basket, ensuring they do not overlap.

4. Cook for 7 minutes, then flip the tenderloins and cook for an additional 7-8 minutes for medium-rare, or adjust the cooking time to your preferred doneness.

5. Let the tenderloins rest for 5 minutes before slicing.

**Number of servings:** 2

**Preparation time:** 10 minutes

**Cooking time:** 15 minutes

**Nutritional value per serving:** Calories: 320, Carbs: 0g, Fiber: 0g, Sugars: 0g, Protein: 48g, Saturated fat: 3g, Unsaturated fat: 5g

**Difficulty rating:** ★★★☆☆

**Tips for ingredient variations:** For a more robust flavor, marinate the venison in a mixture of balsamic vinegar, olive oil, and minced garlic for at least 2 hours before cooking.

# Elk Steak Diane

**Number of servings:** 2

**Preparation time:** 15 minutes

**Cooking time:** 10 minutes

**Nutritional value per serving:** Calories: 410, Carbs: 4g, Fiber: 0g, Sugars: 2g, Protein: 35g, Saturated fat: 18g, Unsaturated fat: 10g

**Difficulty rating:** ★★★★☆

**Tips for ingredient variations:** For a hint of spice, add a dash of cayenne pepper to the sauce.

**Directions:**

1. Season the elk steaks with salt and pepper.

2. Preheat the air fryer to 400°F.

3. Melt one tablespoon of butter in a pan over medium heat. To achieve medium-rare doneness, sear the elk steaks for three minutes on each side. Take out and place the steaks aside.

4. Add the garlic, shallot, and remaining butter to the same skillet. Cook until tender.

5. Add Worcestershire sauce, Dijon mustard, and beef broth and stir. Simmer for three minutes or until the mixture has somewhat reduced.

6. Stir in the heavy cream and simmer for an additional 2 minutes. Season with salt and pepper to taste.

7. Pour the sauce over the elk steaks. Garnish with chopped parsley before serving.

**Ingredients:**

• 2 elk steaks (about 6 oz each)

• 2 tbsp unsalted butter

• 1 shallot, finely chopped

• 1 clove garlic, minced

• 1/4 cup beef broth

• 1 tbsp Worcestershire sauce

• 1 tsp Dijon mustard

• 1/4 cup heavy cream

• Salt and pepper, to taste

• Chopped parsley, for garnish

## Rabbit Roulade

**Ingredients:**

• 1 whole rabbit, deboned and butterflied

• 2 tbsp olive oil

• 1/2 cup spinach, chopped

• 1/4 cup mushrooms, finely chopped

• 2 cloves garlic, minced

• 1/4 cup grated Parmesan cheese

• Salt and pepper, to taste

• Kitchen twine for tying

**Directions:**

1. Preheat the air fryer to 360°F.

2. Season the inside of the rabbit with salt and pepper.

3. In a skillet over medium heat, heat 1 tbsp olive oil. Add spinach, mushrooms, and garlic, sautéing until the spinach is wilted. Remove from heat and let cool slightly.

4. Spread the spinach mixture evenly over the rabbit. Sprinkle with Parmesan cheese.

5. Roll the rabbit tightly and tie with kitchen twine to secure.

6. Rub the outside of the roulade with the remaining olive oil and season with salt and pepper.

7. Place the rabbit roulade in the air fryer basket. Cook for 25 minutes, or until the rabbit is cooked through and the internal temperature reaches 165°F.

8. Let the roulade rest for 10 minutes before removing the twine and slicing.

**Number of servings:** 4

**Preparation time:** 30 minutes

**Cooking time:** 25 minutes

**Nutritional value per serving:** Calories: 320, Carbs: 2g, Fiber: 0.5g, Sugars: 0.5g, Protein: 48g, Saturated fat: 5g, Unsaturated fat: 7g

**Difficulty rating:** ★★★★☆

**Tips for ingredient variations:** Substitute spinach and mushrooms with your choice of filling, such as sun-dried tomatoes, basil, and mozzarella for an Italian twist.

## Goose Breast Roulade

**Number of servings:** 4

**Preparation time:** 20 minutes

**Cooking time:** 40 minutes

**Nutritional value per serving:** Calories: 310, Carbs: 8g, Fiber: 1g, Sugars: 5g, Protein: 45g, Saturated fat: 3g, Unsaturated fat: 5g

**Difficulty rating:** ★★★☆☆

**Tips for ingredient variations:** For a different flavor profile, substitute dried cherries for cranberries or pecans for walnuts.

**Directions:**

1. Preheat the air fryer to 360°F (182°C).

2. Season the flattened goose breasts with salt and pepper.

3. In a bowl, mix together dried cranberries, chopped walnuts, and fresh sage. Spread this mixture over one side of each goose breast.

4. Roll up the goose breasts tightly and secure with kitchen twine.

5. Brush the outside of the roulades with olive oil.

6. Place the goose breast roulades in the air fryer basket and cook for 20 minutes.

7. Pour chicken broth over the roulades and continue cooking for an additional 20 minutes, or until the internal temperature reaches 165°F (74°C).

8. Let the roulades rest for 5 minutes before removing the twine and slicing.

**Ingredients:**

• 2 large goose breasts, flattened

• 1/2 tsp salt

• 1/4 tsp black pepper

• 1/4 cup dried cranberries

• 1/4 cup chopped walnuts

• 2 tbsp chopped fresh sage

• 2 tbsp olive oil

• 1/2 cup chicken broth

## Quail Stuffed with Liver

**Ingredients:**

• 4 quail, cleaned and ready for stuffing

• 1/2 lb chicken liver, finely chopped

• 1/4 cup breadcrumbs

• 1 small onion, finely diced

• 2 cloves garlic, minced

• 2 tbsp fresh parsley, chopped

• 1 tsp thyme

• Salt and pepper, to taste

• 2 tbsp olive oil

**Directions:**

1. Preheat the air fryer to 370°F (188°C).

2. In a skillet over medium heat, sauté the onion and garlic in 1 tablespoon of olive oil until translucent. Add the chicken liver, cooking until just browned.

3. Remove from heat and let cool slightly. Stir in breadcrumbs, parsley, thyme, salt, and pepper.

4. Stuff each quail with the liver mixture, securing the openings with toothpicks.

5. Brush the outside of the stuffed quail with the remaining olive oil.

6. Place the quail in the air fryer basket and cook for 25 minutes, or until the quail are golden brown and cooked through.

7. Serve hot, garnished with additional fresh parsley if desired.

**Number of servings:** 4

**Preparation time:** 30 minutes

**Cooking time:** 25 minutes

**Nutritional value per serving:** Calories: 290, Carbs: 9g, Fiber: 1g, Sugars: 1g, Protein: 27g, Saturated fat: 4g, Unsaturated fat: 6g

**Difficulty rating:** ★★★★☆

**Tips for ingredient variations:** For a richer stuffing, add diced bacon or mushrooms to the liver mixture.

## Lamb Leg Roast

**Number of servings:** 6

**Preparation time:** 15 minutes

**Cooking time:** 60 minutes

**Nutritional value per serving:** Calories: 510, Carbs: 2g, Fiber: 0g, Sugars: 1g, Protein: 76g, Saturated fat: 14g, Unsaturated fat: 22g

**Difficulty rating:** ★★★☆☆

**Tips for ingredient variations:** For a Mediterranean twist, add a tablespoon of chopped olives and a teaspoon of lemon zest to the herb rub.

**Directions:**

1. Preheat the air fryer to 330°F (165°C).

2. Rub the leg of lamb all over with olive oil. Combine the rosemary, thyme, garlic, salt, and pepper in a bowl and rub the mixture onto the lamb.

3. Place the lamb in the air fryer basket and cook for 30 minutes.

4. Mix the red wine and beef broth together and pour over the lamb. Continue cooking for an additional 30 minutes, or until the internal temperature reaches 145°F (63°C) for medium-rare.

5. Let the lamb rest for 10 minutes before slicing.

6. Serve the lamb slices with the cooking juices as a sauce.

**Ingredients:**

• 1 (5 lb) leg of lamb, bone-in

• 2 tbsp olive oil

• 1 tbsp rosemary, minced

• 2 tsp thyme, minced

• 4 cloves garlic, minced

• Salt and pepper, to taste

• 1 cup red wine

• 1/2 cup beef broth

## Beef Tenderloin

**Ingredients:**

- 2 lbs beef tenderloin
- 2 tbsp olive oil
- 1 tsp salt
- 1/2 tsp freshly ground black pepper
- 1 tsp garlic powder
- 1 tsp dried rosemary

**Directions:**

1. Preheat the air fryer to 400°F (204°C).

2. Rub the beef tenderloin with olive oil, then season all sides with salt, black pepper, garlic powder, and dried rosemary.

3. Place the seasoned tenderloin in the air fryer basket.

4. Cook for 30 minutes, or until the tenderloin reaches an internal temperature of 135°F (57°C) for medium-rare. Adjust cooking time for desired doneness.

5. Let the tenderloin rest for 10 minutes before slicing.

**Number of servings:** 4

**Preparation time:** 10 minutes

**Cooking time:** 30 minutes

**Nutritional value per serving:** Calories: 480, Carbs: 0g, Fiber: 0g, Sugars: 0g, Protein: 45g, Saturated fat: 14g, Unsaturated fat: 20g

**Difficulty rating:** ★★★☆☆

**Tips for ingredient variations:** For a smoky flavor, add 1/2 tsp of smoked paprika to the seasoning mix.

---

## Pork Loin with Crackling

**Number of servings:** 4

**Preparation time:** 15 minutes

**Cooking time:** 1 hour

**Nutritional value per serving:** Calories: 520, Carbs: 0g, Fiber: 0g, Sugars: 0g, Protein: 76g, Saturated fat: 9g, Unsaturated fat: 11g

**Difficulty rating:** ★★★★☆

**Tips for ingredient variations:** For an aromatic twist, add a few sprigs of rosemary to the air fryer basket during cooking.

**Directions:**

1. Preheat the air fryer to 360°F (182°C).

2. Score the skin of the pork loin in a diamond pattern. Rub the loin with olive oil, then season generously with sea salt, black pepper, thyme, and minced garlic, ensuring to get the seasoning into the scored skin.

3. Place the pork loin skin side up in the air fryer basket.

4. Cook for 1 hour, or until the skin is crispy and the pork loin reaches an internal temperature of 145°F (63°C).

5. Let the pork loin rest for 10 minutes before slicing, ensuring the crackling is served crispy.

**Ingredients:**

- 2 lbs pork loin, skin on
- 2 tbsp coarse sea salt
- 1 tbsp olive oil
- 1 tsp black pepper
- 1 tsp thyme
- 2 cloves garlic, minced

## Chicken Ballotine

**Ingredients:**

- 1 whole chicken, deboned
- 2 tbsp unsalted butter, softened
- 1 tsp salt
- 1/2 tsp black pepper
- 1/2 cup spinach, chopped
- 1/4 cup grated Parmesan cheese
- 2 cloves garlic, minced
- 1 tsp dried oregano

**Directions:**

1. Preheat the air fryer to 375°F (190°C).

2. Lay the deboned chicken flat, skin side down. Spread the softened butter over the chicken, then season with salt and black pepper.

3. In a bowl, mix together the spinach, Parmesan cheese, minced garlic, and dried oregano. Spread this filling evenly over the chicken.

4. Roll the chicken tightly and tie it with kitchen twine to secure.

5. Place the chicken ballotine in the air fryer basket.

6. Cook for 45 minutes, or until the chicken is golden brown and reaches an internal temperature of 165°F (74°C).

7. Let the chicken ballotine rest for 10 minutes before removing the twine and slicing.

**Number of servings:** 4

**Preparation time:** 20 minutes

**Cooking time:** 45 minutes

**Nutritional value per serving:**
Calories: 320, Carbs: 2g, Fiber: 0.5g, Sugars: 0.5g, Protein: 48g, Saturated fat: 8g, Unsaturated fat: 5g

**Difficulty rating:** ★★★★☆

**Tips for ingredient variations:**
For a different filling, substitute spinach and Parmesan with sautéed mushrooms and Swiss cheese.

## Duck à l'Orange

**Number of servings:** 4

**Preparation time:** 20 minutes

**Cooking time:** 40 minutes

**Nutritional value per serving:**
Calories: 450, Carbs: 22g, Fiber: 1g, Sugars: 18g, Protein: 35g, Saturated fat: 5g, Unsaturated fat: 10g

**Difficulty rating:** ★★★☆☆

**Tips for ingredient variations:**
Substitute honey with maple syrup for a different sweetness or add a splash of brandy to the sauce for depth.

**Directions:**

1. Preheat the air fryer to 360°F (182°C).

2. Score the duck skin in a diamond pattern and season both sides with salt and pepper.

3. Place the duck breasts skin side down in the air fryer basket. Cook for 20 minutes.

4. Flip the duck breasts and cook for an additional 10 minutes, or until the internal temperature reaches 165°F (74°C).

5. While the duck is cooking, combine orange juice, honey, soy sauce, and grated ginger in a saucepan over medium heat. Bring to a simmer.

6. Add the orange segments to the saucepan and cook for 2 minutes.

7. After adding the cornstarch mixture, simmer for an additional two to three minutes, or until the sauce thickens.

8. Once the duck is cooked, let it rest for 5 minutes, then slice.

9. Serve the duck slices topped with the orange sauce.

**Ingredients:**

- 4 duck breasts, skin on
- Salt and pepper, to taste
- 1 cup orange juice
- 2 tablespoons honey
- 1 tablespoon soy sauce
- 1 teaspoon grated ginger
- 2 oranges, peeled and segments cut out
- 1 tablespoon cornstarch mixed with 2 tablespoons water

## Mixed Organ Meat Stew

**Ingredients:**

• 1 lb mixed organ meats (heart, liver, kidney), cubed

• 2 tablespoons olive oil

• 1 large onion, chopped

• 2 carrots, diced

• 2 celery stalks, diced

• 4 garlic cloves, minced

• 1 cup red wine

• 4 cups beef broth

• 2 bay leaves

• 1 teaspoon thyme

• Salt and pepper, to taste

**Directions:**

1. Preheat the air fryer to 390°F (200°C) if it has a roast or bake function.

2. Warm the olive oil in a big frying pan over medium flame. Add the organ meats and cook until browned on all sides. Transfer to the air fryer basket.

3. In the same skillet, add the onion, carrots, celery, and garlic. Cook until softened, about 5 minutes. Transfer the vegetables to the air fryer basket with the meats.

4. Deglaze the skillet with red wine, scraping up any browned bits. Pour the wine over the meats and vegetables in the air fryer.

5. Add beef broth, bay leaves, thyme, salt, and pepper to the air fryer basket.

6. Cook in the air fryer for 2 hours, or until the meats are tender and the stew has thickened.

7. Serve hot, garnished with fresh parsley if desired.

**Number of servings:** 6

**Preparation time:** 30 minutes

**Cooking time:** 2 hours

**Nutritional value per serving:** Calories: 310, Carbs: 8g, Fiber: 2g, Sugars: 3g, Protein: 25g, Saturated fat: 4g, Unsaturated fat: 5g

**Difficulty rating:** ★★★★☆

**Tips for ingredient variations:** Add potatoes or turnips for a heartier stew, or swap red wine with beef stock for a non-alcoholic version.

---

## Bison Ribs

**Number of servings:** 4

**Preparation time:** 15 minutes

**Cooking time:** 3 hours

**Nutritional value per serving:** Calories: 480, Carbs: 20g, Fiber: 1g, Sugars: 15g, Protein: 35g, Saturated fat: 9g, Unsaturated fat: 11g

**Difficulty rating:** ★★★☆☆

**Tips for ingredient variations:** For a spicier version, add 1 teaspoon of cayenne pepper to the spice mix or use a spicy barbecue sauce.

**Directions:**

1. Preheat the air fryer to 250°F (121°C) if it has a slow cook function.

2. In a small bowl, mix together brown sugar, paprika, garlic powder, onion powder, salt, and black pepper.

3. Rub the spice mixture all over the bison ribs.

4. Place the ribs in the air fryer basket. Cook for 2.5 hours.

5. Brush the ribs with barbecue sauce and cook for an additional 30 minutes, or until the ribs are tender and the sauce is caramelized.

6. Serve hot, garnished with additional barbecue sauce if desired.

**Ingredients:**

• 2 lbs bison ribs

• 2 tablespoons brown sugar

• 1 tablespoon paprika

• 1 teaspoon garlic powder

• 1 teaspoon onion powder

• 1 teaspoon salt

• 1/2 teaspoon black pepper

• 1 cup barbecue sauce

## Cedar Plank Salmon

**Ingredients:**

• 1 cedar plank (soaked in water for 1 hour)

• 2 salmon fillets (6 oz each)

• 2 tbsp olive oil

• 1 tsp sea salt

• 1/2 tsp ground black pepper

• 1 lemon, sliced

• 2 sprigs fresh dill

**Directions:**

1. Preheat the air fryer to 400°F.

2. Place the soaked cedar plank in the bottom of the air fryer basket.

3. Add a little olive oil to each salmon fillet and season with black pepper and sea salt.

4. Place the salmon fillets on the cedar plank and top each with lemon slices and a sprig of dill.

5. Make sure the salmon is cooked through and flake readily with a fork by cooking it for 15 minutes in the air fryer.

6. Carefully remove the cedar plank from the air fryer and serve the salmon directly from the plank.

**Number of servings:** 2

**Preparation time:** 10 minutes (plus 1 hour for soaking the cedar plank)

**Cooking time:** 15 minutes

**Nutritional value per serving:** Calories: 345, Carbs: 1g, Fiber: 0g, Sugars: 0g, Protein: 34g, Saturated fat: 5g, Unsaturated fat: 15g

**Difficulty rating:** ★★☆☆☆

**Tips for ingredient variations:** For a smoky flavor, sprinkle smoked paprika on the salmon before cooking. For a citrusy note, add orange slices in addition to lemon.

## Stuffed Trout

**Number of servings:** 2

**Preparation time:** 20 minutes

**Cooking time:** 15 minutes

**Nutritional value per serving:** Calories: 410, Carbs: 6g, Fiber: 3g, Sugars: 1g, Protein: 34g, Saturated fat: 10g, Unsaturated fat: 15g

**Difficulty rating:** ★★★☆☆

**Tips for ingredient variations:** For added flavor, mix in diced sun-dried tomatoes or capers with the stuffing.

**Directions:**

1. Preheat the air fryer to 380°F.

2. In a small bowl, mix together almond flour, chopped walnuts, melted butter, minced garlic, and chopped parsley. Season with salt and pepper.

3. Stuff each trout with the almond flour mixture, pressing gently to fill.

4. Place the stuffed trout in the air fryer basket, ensuring they do not overlap.

5. Cook for 15 minutes, or until the trout is cooked through and the stuffing is golden brown.

6. Serve immediately with lemon wedges on the side.

**Ingredients:**

• 2 whole trout, cleaned and gutted

• 1/4 cup almond flour

• 1/4 cup finely chopped walnuts

• 2 tbsp unsalted butter, melted

• 1 tsp minced garlic

• 1/4 cup chopped parsley

• Salt and pepper, to taste

• Lemon wedges, for serving

## Grilled Shark Steaks

**Ingredients:**

- 2 shark steaks (about 6 oz each)
- 1/4 cup soy sauce
- 2 tbsp olive oil
- 1 tbsp lemon juice
- 2 tsp minced garlic
- 1 tsp dried oregano
- Salt and pepper, to taste

**Directions:**

1. In a bowl, whisk together soy sauce, olive oil, lemon juice, minced garlic, and dried oregano. Season with salt and pepper.

2. Marinate the shark steaks in the mixture for at least 30 minutes in the refrigerator.

3. Preheat the air fryer to 400°F.

4. Remove the shark steaks from the marinade and place them in the air fryer basket, ensuring they do not overlap.

5. Cook for 10 minutes, flipping halfway through, until the steaks are cooked through and slightly charred on the edges.

6. Serve immediately, garnished with additional lemon wedges if desired.

**Number of servings:** 2

**Preparation time:** 15 minutes (plus marinating time)

**Cooking time:** 10 minutes

**Nutritional value per serving:** Calories: 280, Carbs: 2g, Fiber: 0g, Sugars: 0g, Protein: 40g, Saturated fat: 3g, Unsaturated fat: 5g

**Difficulty rating:** ★★★☆☆

**Tips for ingredient variations:** For a spicy version, add a pinch of red pepper flakes to the marinade. For an Asian twist, substitute lemon juice with lime juice and add a splash of fish sauce.

## Broiled Swordfish

**Number of servings:** 2

**Preparation time:** 10 minutes

**Cooking time:** 12 minutes

**Nutritional value per serving:** Calories: 280, Carbs: 0g, Fiber: 0g, Sugars: 0g, Protein: 34g, Saturated fat: 4g, Unsaturated fat: 8g

**Difficulty rating:** ★★☆☆☆

**Tips for ingredient variations:** For a spicy twist, add a pinch of cayenne pepper to the olive oil mixture before coating the swordfish.

**Directions:**

1. Preheat the air fryer to 400°F using the broil setting if available.

2. Brush both sides of the swordfish steaks with olive oil. Season with oregano, lemon zest, salt, and pepper.

3. Place the swordfish steaks in the air fryer basket, ensuring they do not overlap.

4. Cook for 6 minutes, then flip the steaks and cook for an additional 6 minutes, or until the steaks are cooked through and slightly golden on the outside.

5. Serve immediately, garnished with additional lemon zest if desired.

**Ingredients:**

- 2 swordfish steaks (about 6 oz each)
- 2 tbsp olive oil
- 1 tsp dried oregano
- 1 tsp lemon zest
- Salt and pepper, to taste

## Seared Tuna with Avocado

**Ingredients:**

• 2 tuna steaks (about 6 oz each)

• 1 tbsp soy sauce

• 1 tbsp olive oil

• 1/2 tsp ground ginger

• Salt and pepper, to taste

• 1 ripe avocado, sliced

• 1 tsp sesame seeds

• 1 tbsp lime juice

**Directions:**

1. In a small bowl, mix together soy sauce, olive oil, ground ginger, salt, and pepper.

2. Rub the mixture over both sides of the tuna steaks.

3. Preheat the air fryer to 400°F.

4. Place the tuna steaks in the air fryer basket, ensuring they do not overlap.

5. Cook for 2 minutes, then flip the steaks and cook for an additional 2 minutes for rare, or adjust the cooking time to your preferred doneness.

6. Arrange the sliced avocado on plates. Place the seared tuna on top of the avocado slices.

7. Sprinkle sesame seeds over the tuna and drizzle with lime juice before serving.

**Number of servings:** 2

**Preparation time:** 15 minutes

**Cooking time:** 4 minutes

**Nutritional value per serving:**
Calories: 310, Carbs: 9g, Fiber: 7g, Sugars: 1g, Protein: 31g, Saturated fat: 3g, Unsaturated fat: 13g

**Difficulty rating:** ★★★☆☆

**Tips for ingredient variations:**
For an extra kick, mix a pinch of chili powder into the soy sauce mixture before coating the tuna.

# Conclusion

Celebrating your success with the Carnivore Diet Air Fryer Cookbook marks a pivotal moment in your health and culinary journey. You've embraced a lifestyle that prioritizes high-quality, nutrient-dense meats prepared in ways that maximize both flavor and health benefits. Through this book, you've discovered the power of simplicity in eating, the profound impact of a meat-centric diet on your well-being, and the versatility of your air fryer as a tool for transforming simple cuts of meat into culinary masterpieces.

The Carnivore Diet, with its focus on meat, challenges conventional dietary norms and offers a path to improved health that many find liberating. It's a testament to the idea that nourishing your body with the foods it was designed to thrive on can lead to significant improvements in energy, mental clarity, and overall vitality. This book has equipped you with the knowledge to select the best cuts of meat, understand their nutritional value, and prepare them in ways that preserve and enhance their benefits.

Your air fryer has become more than just an appliance; it's a gateway to efficient, healthy cooking. The recipes and techniques shared in these pages have shown you how to achieve the perfect balance of crispy and tender, all while maintaining the nutritional integrity of your meals. The convenience and speed of air frying mean that even the busiest individuals can stick to the Carnivore Diet without sacrificing taste or variety.

Beyond the recipes, this book has aimed to foster a deeper understanding of the Carnivore Diet's principles and benefits. You've learned about the historical and evolutionary basis for a meat-focused diet, how it can be a tool for reversing common health issues, and the importance of community and support in maintaining this lifestyle. The anecdotes and case studies have hopefully served as inspiration, showing that real, transformative health outcomes are possible.

As you continue on your carnivore journey, remember that this book is not just a collection of recipes but a resource for ongoing learning and exploration. The Carnivore Diet is highly personal, and what works for one person may not work for another. Use this book as a foundation to experiment, adjust, and find what makes you feel your best. The ultimate goal is not just to follow a diet but to live a lifestyle that brings you health, happiness, and satisfaction.

Looking ahead, the world of carnivore eating and air frying is ever-evolving. New research, techniques, and recipes are continually emerging, offering fresh insights and inspiration. Stay curious, open to trying new things, and connected to the carnivore community. Your journey is unique, and every meal is an opportunity to nourish your body, delight your taste buds, and celebrate the simple joy of eating well.

Thank you for choosing the Carnivore Diet Air Fryer Cookbook as your companion on this journey. Here's to many more delicious, nourishing meals prepared in your air fryer, and to your continued health and well-being.

# INDEX

Made in United States
Troutdale, OR
09/23/2024

23045781R00046